MW00508879

THE MONSTER CALLED DIVORCE

The Greatest Tragedy Of Modern-Day Families

JULIE D.A OGUARA (ESQ)

Copyright © 2022 by Julie D.A Oguara (ESQ)
ISBN: Paperback   978-1-956096-52-1
            eBook   978-1-956096-53-8

LCCN : 2022903268

All rights reserved. No part of this publication may be reproduced, distributed, or transmitted in any form or by any electronic or mechanical means, without the prior written permission of the publisher, except in the case of brief quotations embodied in critical reviews and certain other noncommercial uses permitted by copyright law.

Printed in the United States of America

To God Almighty who gave me the vision and ability to pen it down. To you alone be all the glory.

To my late loving, wonderful, and caring parents, Elder Clifford T. Amgbara and Evangelist (Mrs.) Olive T. Amgbara, without whom I may never have understood the power of true love and marriage.

To my children, Telimoye (Jnr), Ebiteinye, Eneni, and Wanaemi, whom God took his time to create fearfully and wonderfully. You are indeed my joy and pride. I cannot tell you enough how much I love you. You are, of all things, a great blessing from God.

CONTENTS

ACKNOWLEDGEMENTS

There are so many wonderful people who contributed in immeasurable ways to my experience in writing this book. A lot of people seemed to be dealing with extra burdens brought on you by challenges in your families and relationships. I wanted to get this book out there to encourage you and give you hope and inspiration. I felt it is important to remind every one of you that you are not alone, not as long as you have faith.

My gratitude to my children, siblings, and relations who, though unknown to you, through your actions and comments, generously brought about this work. I will always appreciate your love and support.

My heartfelt gratitude to some of my domestic and office staff, Bridget Ogechi Nwamulo and Patrick Ifeanyi Onyemaobi, who worked tirelessly for me when writing this book. I appreciate you so much.

Thank you to my editing team, who facilitated the editing of this work, Edwin Inibi who helped me coordinate this project, Samuel I. Kalaiyo, and Onengi Kalaiyo. Your hard work, vision, and encouragement have immensely influenced this book and, consequently, my life.

A special note of appreciation to Jane Help-Yawei, producer, *Sunday Delight*, Bayelsa State Radio—a programme in which I was a guest for six months discussing issues affecting the family and society. Also my appreciation goes to Lauretta N. Konugah, the producer of *Family and Society* (my programme) on Radio Nigeria, Treasure FM, Port Harcourt, Rivers State. These programmes opened my eyes greatly to the challenges people go through in their families.

Thank you to my numerous listeners who have encouraged and supported me through your telephone calls, text messages, e-mails, etc. Though I have never met most of you personally, I appreciate all your suggestions and contributions.

Collins Edebiri, my mentor, your support and tenacity indeed started the ball rolling.

Thank you, Emmanuel K. Ogonnaya, Koke E. Ogbonnaya, Chimnomnso O. Ogbonnaya, and Kwerechukwu N. Ogbonnaya. Your prayers, love, and years have kept my children and I through those years of our wilderness sojourn. You are a wonderful family. I love you so much.

Special thanks as well to my friends, Christie Oloko and Wisdom Abraham, who in no little way pushed me to answer to what God has called me to do.

I also want to acknowledge the compassion and encouragement that I consistently received from my church family. My special thanks goes to my former resident minister, Jacob M. B. Ibikunle; the assistant resident minister (Port Harcourt), Mba Idika; and the former president of the women's league, Boma Bob-Manuel and all the members of the league for giving me the opportunity to speak to the women during the Mothering Sunday Week Programme 2011. This afforded me an opportunity to speak to some members of my church family on the issue of divorce and how it should be perceived and handled in a family.

To all who invited me to speak at various times and different occasions on the consequences of divorce after the first publication of this book, those who attended conferences organized by my NGO, listened to my radio programmes, read the book and gave your comments that have birthed this second edition, I am most grateful. Thank you for your immeasurable contributions.

Michael Ebenezer Briggs, I cannot thank you enough for your numerous hours of typing this project manuscript. Nath Excellence, Timi Pere, Sokari Pepple and Obiajulu Amuamuziam, you added finishing touches to the already-typed manuscript. It was indeed an added polish; you are appreciated.

Finally, to Agarwood Publishing, you treated my work and me with great respect and integrity. My gratitude to Anthony Adeiyi, the manager of Inter-Sop Press and Publishers.

INTRODUCTION

I had so much pain in my heart each time I came across families that were unstable. I could never imagine the pains they went through because I had great, caring, and loving parents. All that I knew about family life was love, peace, and joy. There must have been moments of slight disagreements, but I never knew about such while growing up. My family home was a place of solace and refuge. A few friends I grew up with whose families were not as stable as mine, could not understand why I was so green each time they talked about what was going on in their homes. It was strange to me. All that I can remember as I write is that I encouraged them to be strong and forge ahead with life. My parents assisted some financially, materially, and emotionally each time they got to know about the problems of those few friends of mine. Emphasis is on the word *few* because I rarely came across people with dysfunctional families in those days as I see all around today. Or it might be because I was too comfortable and did not observe what was happening around me. I never knew that my children would have a story completely different from mine. My desire to speak against the alarming rate of divorce, separation, and cohabitation burnt in me when in 1997, I had a personal experience of being thrown out of my matrimonial home despite all my pleading to be allowed to stay; though not divorced. I was later appointed as the legal adviser for five years to the then Ministry of Women Affairs in Bayelsa

State of Nigeria in the same year. This appointment was an eye-opener as well as a heart breaker for me.

It was then I realized how families are in trouble. I counselled a lot of couples and, to the glory of God, those marriages were saved. The question then was, why should God use me to settle the marriages of others while mine was in a mess? I never knew my mess would become my message. I became disillusioned and was almost getting angry at God. Can you imagine me getting angry at God? But that was how I really felt.

As the years passed by, I knew without any doubt that God had an assignment and a purpose for me. Maybe he allowed what had happened to my family for this reason. He talked to me audibly several times to go on radio and television to do programmes on the family. I refused and saw myself as most unfit for the assignment. This I mentioned to a few people. Also, there were several times that I came in contact with people who said, "Do you know you have a call of God in your life?" I knew it but was always in denial because, to me, that could not be for me.

In 2010, I reluctantly commenced my assignment by featuring in a programme on Radio Bayelsa that had its hostess as Mrs. Jane Help-Yawei for six months. This was a programme which touched and healed several families and I thought this was the end but I was wrong. God later gave me several titles of books to write. This book, *The Monster Called Divorce* is just the beginning of more to come.

In December 2011, the programme *Family and* Society, which is my programme, began featuring every Sunday afternoon on Radio Nigeria, Treasure FM, Port Harcourt, Rivers State. This programme was on for several years touching a lot of souls and healing families.

This book, *The Monster Called Divorce is* written in six chapters. Each chapter is designed to build on the other. It begins with a chapter titled "Nature of Marriage" because we cannot discuss the issue of divorce without going through the journey of marriage. "Nature of Marriage" talks of the origin of marriage. The chapter also discusses the different types of marriages as recognised by law in Nigeria, most other African countries and some other countries around the world. The laws governing these types of marriages vary from one country to another though the principles are similar in nature.

However, the book, *The Monster Called Divorce*, is aimed at identifying what constitutes a "monster" that may result in the divorce of parties in a marriage. Divorce is a universal phenomenon which I intend to discuss later in the book. It is therefore not peculiar to a particular nation or region of the globe despite the type of marriage entered into by spouses.

It is an eye-opener for anyone reading this book to have a better understanding of what marriage is, especially in Nigeria.

"Why Marry" is the next chapter that talks of some of the reasons people give to explain why they get married. Are the reasons given all good or bad? The chapter seeks to encourage us to know some of the reasons why people get married and to enable one to choose a life partner that would not later become one's doom in life because of a wrong reason or reasons.

"The Monster" is obviously where the issue of divorce and what causes divorce are elaborately discussed. So many couples are ignorant of the ways this "monster" operates. The goal is to help you prevent the deadly monster from slowly creeping into your home after marriage. This also serves as a tool for grandmas, grandpas as well as parents to help their children before or in the course of their marriage if and when needed.

"Factors Inhibiting the Success of Marriage—Sociological Perspective" is the fourth chapter that talks of certain factors inhibiting the success of marriage in our society today. These are discussed from a sociological perspective based on research findings and my experience during counselling sessions with some of my clients.

In"The Web", which is the fifth chapter, the consequences of divorce as it affects the parties—offspring of the marriage, friends, relations, and the society at large—are handled.

Finally, the book concludes with the chapter on "Fix It". We make mistakes in life. We have the strength to change for good if we are willing. This chapter will motivate you to step into your change for a better family life and society. Stay open to something new and good. Find your place of blessing to your family and the society in general.

As marriage is not intended to be the graveyard of any man or woman, so should all apply wisdom to see that it succeeds. Where it fails is when all that needs to be done by the willing spouse is done, keep your heart pure, strive for excellence, and prepare yourself because God's goodness, favour, and restoration will be your portion. Marriage is meant to be enjoyed and be a blessing to those in it, their offspring and the entire society. It is your time to walk in the fullness and purpose of God in creating the institution of marriage.

Julie D.A. Oguara(Esq)

CHAPTER ONE

NATURE OF MARRIAGE

We must not start by wondering why I have decided to discuss marriage rather than divorce as expected in this book. There is no structure or a house that is built without a foundation that will stand. There must, of necessity, be a foundation, no matter how weak, to start the building of a house. This is my reason for delving into the basics of what marriage is.

MARRIAGE AS ORDAINED BY GOD

After creation, God saw that all living creatures were created as male and female, except man. He saw that the man could not effectively relate with all other animals and was very lonely and that he needed a companion despite the beauty around him.

And the Lord God caused a deep sleep to fall upon Adam, and he slept: and he took one of his ribs. And the rib which the Lord God had taken from man; made he a woman, and brought her unto the man.

And Adam said;

> This is now bone of my bones, and flesh of my flesh; she shall be called woman, because she was taken out of man. Therefore shall a man leave his father and his mother, and shall cleave unto his wife: and they shall be one flesh. (Genesis 2:21-24)

It is God's intention that the man and his wife should experience oneness in their marriage relationship.

MARRIAGE AS A UNIVERSAL INSTITUTION

Marriage is a universal institution that is recognised and respected all over the world. As a social institution, marriage is founded on, and governed by, the social and religious norms of a society. Consequently, the sanctity of marriage is a well-accepted principle in the world community. Marriage is the root of the family and society. Marriage, though a social institution, is also guided by laws (when applicable) of the community in which they operate. This simply means that depending on the type of marriage the parties to a marriage enter into, the world community has its laws guiding the parties involved to ensure some form of order in the society. I intend to view marriage from the social, religious, and legal perspectives to enable you to appreciate later as you read on, why I went on a voyage to write this book, *The Monster Called Divorce*.

WHAT IS MARRIAGE?

It is universally accepted that marriage is a union of a man and a woman, which involves two persons of opposite sex. This fundamental principle is, however, being challenged now as a result of transsexual operations in countries such as the United States of America, Canada and some other western countries, as well as the existence of hermaphrodites and pseudohermaphrodites.

In this work, I am not going to concern myself with the latter— that is, transsexual operations, hermaphrodites, pseudoher-maphrodites and same sex marriage. As had been stated earlier, marriage, from its origin, was intended for a man and a woman (Genesis 2:22-23).

In my country, Nigeria, the law recognizes three (3) types of marriages; viz

    a   the monogamous marriage (also known as the statutory marriage or court marriage);

    b   polygamous marriage (otherwise referred to as customary marriage); and

    c   Islamic law marriage.

In general, there are two types of marriages; Civil and religious marriage. It is however worthy of note that there are several other types being practiced by various societies around the globe. These are:

    a   Polygyny—This type of marriage is characterized by one man married to several wives at the same time. It is similar to Non Sororal Polygyny in some societies and polygamous marriage in Nigeria;

though different in how the ceremonies are done during the marriage.

b   Polyandry:
   i   Fraternal Polyandry
   ii   Non Fraternal Polyandry
c   Sororal Polygyny
d   Monogamy—This is also known as Civil marriage in most western countries, statutory marriage or Court marriage in Nigeria.
e   Serial Monogamy
f   Group marriage

In this work, we are going to concern ourselves with the monogamous system of marriage and the polygamous marriage system, excluding but without prejudices, other types of marriage.

MONOGAMOUS MARRIAGE

In Nigeria and most African countries, monogamous marriage is the same as in England. This is the marriage which was described by Lord Penzance in the celebrated case of *Hyde v. Hyde* as "the voluntary union for life of one man and one woman to the exclusion of all others". In order for a marriage to be a valid monogamous marriage, there must be the existence of three major characteristics. This simply means that, firstly, the parties to the intended marriage must enter into the same voluntarily. There must be free and genuine consent of both parties. The second arm is that the marriage is intended to be for life. This does not mean that the union cannot be dissolved but that at the time of entering into the marriage relationship, parties intend it to be for life unless dissolved earlier by a process prescribed by law. Thirdly, but not the least, that it must be a union of one man and one woman to the exclusion of all others. It therefore means that as long as the marriage subsists, neither of the parties can be married to another person. If another marriage is contracted, it constitutes the offence of bigamy.

This definition of a monogamous marriage by Lord Penzance is in harmony with God's intention when he created the institution of marriage from the beginning. God said, "Therefore shall a man leave his father and his mother, and shall cleave unto his wife: and they shall be one flesh" (Genesis 2:24).

The principles governing monogamous marriage in most countries of the world where it is practiced are similar though the applicable laws differ. In Nigeria, the Marriage Act enacted in 1914; Cap M6 Laws of the Federation of Nigeria, 2004; and the Matrimonial Causes Act No. 18, 1970, Cap M7 Laws of the Federation of Nigeria 2004 apply.

ESSENTIAL REQUIREMENTS FOR A VALID MONOGAMOUS MARRIAGE

1. Age

Age is an important aspect in contracting a marriage. A marriage is void where either one or both parties are not of marriageable age. However, the law in Nigeria did not define in our law what marriageable age is. Nonetheless, in Nigeria, the age is usually presumed to be the age of puberty.

It should however be noted that the legal age of marriage in most countries at present is between the age of 18 and 21 years.

Any person below the 18 years of age, requires parental consent in most cases.

A lot could be written on the aspect of marriage based on parental consent due to either one or both parties to the marriage not attaining the majority age of marriage. However, since this book is not dealing with marriage in the strict sense of the word but the monster called divorce, I would rather not bother you with that issue in this book.

2. **Sanity**

It is necessary to ascertain that parties intending to contract a statutory marriage are not insane. The purpose is to ensure that either or both parties have the mental capacity to understand the nature and consequences of the transaction to be entered into by them. If one of the parties is insane, it renders the marriage void ab initio (from the beginning).

3. **Prohibited Degrees of Consanguinity and Affinity**

There is a general rule that persons contracting a statutory marriage must not be within the prohibited degrees of consanguinity or affinity. Therefore, marriage between the prohibited degrees of consanguinity and affinity is void.

This means that under the Marriage Act, a person cannot marry his or her ancestor, descendant, sister, brother, father's sister or father's brother, son or daughter, brother's or sister's son, mother's brother or sister, and brother's or sister's daughter. Marriage is also prohibited on the ground of affinity between a man and his wife's mother, wife's grandmother, wife's sister, wife's son's daughter, wife's daughter's daughter, father's wife, grandfather's wife, son's wife, son's and daughter's son's wife. The reverse position applies to the woman. It is immaterial whether the relationship is of the whole blood or half blood.

However, section 4 of the Matrimonial Causes Act 1970 enables two persons within the prohibited degrees of affinity who wish to marry to apply in writing to a high court judge of law for permission to do so. The judge may by order permit the applicants to get married if he is satisfied that the circumstances of the particular case are so exceptional as to justify the granting of the permission sought. An example of such exceptional circumstances is when a man and a woman who are related (without knowing that they are so related) get into a relationship with a child as an end product. This can constitute an exceptional circumstance. Reasons such as parties merely being in love are not sufficient, and as such, a marriage can be declared void. It is worthy of note, however, that the procedure before granting the permit by a judge after a written application of permit by the applicants is very cumbersome.

4. Consent

Marriage being a voluntary union of the parties as earlier discussed, it is imperative that parties consent freely to it. Absence of consent, or the obtaining of the same by duress or fraud, vitiates the marriage. The Marriage Act in Nigeria specifically provides that where one of the parties of the marriage is less than twenty-one years of age, parental consent is needed.

Consent of parents is also needed as earlier stated, by intending couples of other jurisdictions outside Nigeria; where either of the parties or both are below the ages of 18 and 21 years.

5. Single Status

It is essential that the parties to a monogamous or statutory marriage must at the time of celebration of the marriage have a single status. If either of them is in a subsisting marriage with a third party, that is, a statutory marriage or customary law marriage (which would be discussed later in this book). The celebration of the subsequent statutory marriage constitutes a criminal offence of bigamy.

The exception to this rule is that parties who are already married under customary law can marry themselves under the Marriage Act. It should, however, be noted that where a man under the customary law is married to more than one wife, he may validly contract a statutory marriage with one of the numerous wives or a third party provided the other marriages are properly dissolved customarily.

FORMAL VALIDITY OF A STATUTORY MARRIAGE

The Marriage Act in Nigeria lays down certain preliminary formalities which are to be fulfilled before the solemnization of marriage under the act. Although, the various step-by-step formalities as practised in Nigeria stated below are not the same with what obtains in other parts of the world, every country has a formal procedure for a valid statutory marriage.

1. Notice of Marriage

As a first step, parties who intend to be married under the Marriage Act must give notice of their intended marriage to the registrar of marriage in the marriage district where the marriage is intended to take place. This is done by either of the parties that reside in the said district by completing and signing the prescribed form and payment of the prescribed fee. The registrar then enters the details in the marriage notice book. The notice is subsequently displayed on the public notice board outside the registrar's office for twenty-one working days but before the expiration of three months from the date of the notice. The display of the notice remains until the registrar issues the registrar's certificate at the expiration of the twenty-one working days or before the three months expire as the case may be. Inspection of the marriage notice book is open to the general public during working hours without a fee.

It is, however, worthy of note that the marriage must take place within three months of the date of notice. Failure to comply with this requirement makes the notice and all proceedings consequent thereupon void. The parties who find themselves in such circumstances must give a fresh notice if they still desire to contract a valid marriage.

2. Special Licence

The prescribed procedure of notice of marriage and the issuance of the registrar's certificate can be dispensed with in some cases, if the governor of a state is satisfied with the circumstances of a particular case. Under this procedure, the parties must swear to an affidavit which the governor thereof will have the right to grant his own licence to the applicants, given that he is satisfied that there is no lawful impediment to the proposed marriage and the necessary consent, if any, to the proposed marriage has been obtained.

Special licence is granted inter alia, where the parties cannot wait for the prescribed twenty-one days after the notice with the registrar. Also, such special licence is mostly granted where a public figure desires to contract a marriage quietly without publicity.

3. Caveat

Where a notice of marriage has been displayed, anyone who knows of any just cause why the marriage should not be celebrated can enter a caveat. The caveat is entered by the aggrieved party writing the word "Forbidden" opposite the entry of the notice of the marriage notice book and appending the writer's name, address, and the ground on which the person claims to forbid the issue of the registrar's certificate. The registrar can on the verbal instruction of such a person enter the caveat where the caveator or caveatrix is an *illiterate* on behalf of that person in the marriage notice book. Once this is done, the registrar may not issue his certificate until the caveat is removed.

The law in that case requires the registrar to refer the matter to a judge of the high court of the state. If the judge is satisfied that the grounds for opposing the issuance of the certificate are insufficient, he may remove the caveat by cancelling the word "Forbidden" in the marriage notice book and writing the words "Cancelled by order of the high court" below the entry and sign his name.

The registrar then issues his certificate and the marriage may proceed as if no caveat was entered. The grounds on which a caveat may be successfully entered include that one of the parties to the contended marriage is already married to a third party either under the Marriage Act or customary law. It should be noted that mere engagement or betrothal of one party to a third party is not enough.

Another point of note is that a caveator or caveatrix who is not satisfied with the ruling of a high court judge has a right of appeal up to the supreme court.

4. Registrar's Certificate

The registrar may, after twenty-one days or before the expiration of three months from the date of notice on the payment of the prescribed fees, issue his certificate to the applicants. The registrar may issue his certificate when he is satisfied that by the affidavit of the applicants

i) one of the parties to the intended marriage has been resident within the marriage district in which it is intended to be celebrated for at least fifteen days preceding the granting of the certificate;

ii) each of the parties, if not a widow or a widower, is twenty-one years old, or where he or she is under the age of twenty-one, the required consent has been obtained in writing and attached to the affidavit;

iii) there is no impediment of consanguinity or affinity or any other lawful hindrance to the marriage; and

iv) Neither of the parties to the intended marriage is married by customary law to any person other than the person with whom such marriage proposed is to be contracted.

The said affidavit may be sworn to before a registrar or an administrative officer or a recognised minister of religion. The law requires the person taking such an affidavit to explain to the maker what the prohibited degrees of consanguinity and affinity are. He also has the responsibility of explaining the imposed penalty by law for contracting marriage under the Marriage Act with a third party while there is a subsistent customary law marriage or contracting marriage by customary law when already married under the act. Failure to make these explanations is punishable with imprisonment for two years. The person making the explanation must also sign a declaration that he has given the required explanation and that the maker of the affidavit appeared to fully understand it.

5. **Celebration of Marriage**

When the parties of an intended marriage have obtained either a registrar's certificate or a special license, they may be married in one of two different ways:

a) **MARRIAGE IN A LICENSED PLACE OF WORSHIP**

The governor of a state has the power to license certain places of public worship within his state for the celebration of marriages. Such a license may also be revoked. The parties may have their marriage celebrated in a licensed place of worship by any recognised minister of the church, denomination, or body to which such a place of worship belongs. The marriage must be celebrated between 8:00 a.m. and 6:00 p.m. Note that a marriage performed by a person who is not a recognised minister of a religious organisation in which the marriage is celebrated is void. The officiating minister can also celebrate a marriage in a place mentioned in a special license.

It is also mandatory that he should not solemnize a marriage until the parties thereto deliver to him the registrar's certificate or a special license. The officiating minister is required to complete the marriage certificate in triplicate. He is then obliged to hand over one copy of the certificate to the parties. Another copy should be transmitted within seven days to the registrar of marriages within the district in which the marriage took place; otherwise, it would be void. The church keeps one copy. It is very important to note that it is not every church in Nigeria that is authorised or licensed to conduct a statutory marriage.

b) **MARRIAGE IN A REGISTRAR'S OFFICE**

The parties who have obtained a registrar's certificate or a special license may, as an alternative, contract a marriage before a marriage registrar in his office in the presence of at least two witnesses. The celebration of the marriage inter alia must be between 10:00 a.m. and 4:00 p.m. Such marriage celebrated in a registrar's office is valid without the need for any other godly or religious rites. The marriage cannot be dissolved except by the decree of a high court, and it is an offence of bigamy for a party to the marriage to contract another marriage during the subsistence of the first one.

c) **MARRIAGE IN NIGERIAN DIPLOMATIC MISSIONS**

Marriage can also be validly celebrated outside Nigeria in a Nigerian diplomatic or consular mission office. It is essential that one of the parties to the marriage is a Nigerian citizen and the marriage must be contracted before a Nigerian diplomatic or consular office of the rank of a secretary or above.

d) MARRIAGE UNDER SPECIAL LICENCE

A special license may authorise the celebration of marriage at a place other than a licensed place of worship or the office of the registrar of marriages, but the marriage must be celebrated by a minister of religion or a registrar.

e) CHURCH MARRIAGE

Various religious denominations in Nigeria celebrate marriages between their members which have no relevance to or connection with the Marriage Act. The church marriage or church blessing does not have any binding legal effect on the parties to a marriage. At best, it is an intended statutory marriage.

For instance, some religious organisations in Nigeria insist that their members who have married otherwise than in accordance with their prescribed religious rites, must have their marriages celebrated either as church marriage or church blessing according to what is applicable to the parties to the intended marriage at the time of the celebration. Such church marriage or church blessing does not constitute any marriage under the act. Where parties to an existing customary law marriage are subsequently blessed in a church, the church blessing or church marriage does not alter the essential customary character of the marriage.

The woman is usually made to keep the marriage certificate as it is always handed over to her after the signing of the marriage certificate as the evidence of the marriage that took place. This is a practice or procedure though not backed up by law.

f) POLYGAMOUS OR CUSTOMARY LAW MARRIAGE

A polygamous or customary law marriage is defined as the voluntary union for life of one man with one or several wives. The main feature of a customary law marriage is the capacity of the man to take more than one wife concurrently as he pleases. The mere fact that at any given time he has only one wife does not affect the character of the marriage, so long as the capacity of taking more wives is retained. The fact that there may be several wives at any given time does not affect a major aspect that a customary law marriage is also intended to last for life.

Polygamy in Nigeria is a customary law institution. The character and incidents of that system are governed by customary law. There is, therefore, no uniform system of customary law prevailing throughout Nigeria. The multitude of systems of law which differ from one locality to another is applicable to the various localities in which they exist. There are essential and formal requirements for the celebration of valid customary law marriages. The details of such requirements vary from one locality to another; however, the broad principles are sometimes similar.

Capacity

The parties to a customary law marriage must possess the capacity under the law to marry each other.

1. Age

Customary law of most localities in Nigeria does not prescribe any age for the solemnization of customary law marriage. This to a large extent has encouraged a high incidence of child marriage with all its attendant evils. While in some areas, child betrothal is rampant, marriage does not in fact take place until the parties have attained the age of puberty. However, in some states of the Federal Republic of Nigeria, the minimum age for customary law marriage has been fixed by legislature. This ranges between twelve years and sixteen years.

2. Consent

Two types of consent are required for the celebration of customary law marriage. These are the consent of the parties and parental consent.

a) Consent of Parties

As a general rule, the consent of the parties to a customary law marriage where they are capable of expressing their consent to the marriage is very important. Where the parties are capable of expressing their consent to the marriage, such consent is expressly demanded and obtained before the marriage; else, such marriage will be void. If a party objects to the marriage, he or she may refuse to go through with the ceremony. Even in those areas of Nigeria where child marriage is still practised, the consent of the parties is required when both parties come of age. Any party who did not in fact consent to the marriage may at any point annul the marriage by abandoning the other party.

b) Parental Consent

Parental consent is necessary and in some cases mandatory for the celebration of a valid customary law marriage. As a support to this general principle is the fact that, to an extent, customary law marriage is viewed as a transaction between two families. The requisite consent is that of the father or guardian to the prospective spouse. Parental consent is mandatory for a girl under customary law system of marriage even where she has attained majority. The reasons are easy to know. It is important because without the consent of her father, for instance, the bride-price cannot be properly paid. Moreover, the formal giving away of the bride may not take place. These are two basic elements for a valid customary law marriage.

However, exceptions to the requirement of parental consent exist in some parts of Nigeria where the parents are adamant to giving their consent without any cogent reason. In such a situation, if the bride- and bridegroom-to-be have attained the age of eighteen or above, they may jointly institute a legal proceeding in a competent court against the parent or guardian to show cause why he or she refuses consent or to accept his or her share of the dowry. If the court is of the opinion that no sufficient cause has been shown, it shall order that the marriage may proceed without the consent of such parent.

The provision above is, however, not without its constraints since the issue of the two constituent elements of customary law marriage of bride-price being properly paid and the formal giving out of the bride may not take place. On the contrary, an adult male may contract a valid marriage without the consent of his parents.

6. Statutory Prohibition

In Nigeria, a person who is a party to an existing statutory marriage or a monogamous marriage recognised by law lacks the capacity during the continuance of such marriage, of contracting a valid customary law marriage to another person.

7. Prohibited Degree of Consanguinity and Affinity

In most systems of customary law marriage in Nigeria, the prohibited degrees of consanguinity for marriage are much wider than those applicable under the Marriage Act discussed earlier in this chapter.

8. Position of Non-Native of Nigeria

It has been decided in cases that a non-Nigerian is not subject to the customary law in Nigeria and therefore has no capacity to contract a valid customary law marriage. A non-Nigerian relation with other persons (Nigerians) can only be governed by English law which does not allow polygamy.

However, this position is slightly different in the northern part of Nigeria since customary law is now applicable to any person whose parents were members of any tribe or tribes indigenous to some part of Africa or one whose parent was a member of such a tribe.

9. Bride-Price

The payment of bride-price is essential for a valid customary law marriage. The basic characteristics of bride-price are as follows:

a) It is a gift or payment which may be in the form of money, natural produce, or some other form of property.
b) The payment must be made to the parent or guardian to the bride-to-be.
c) It must be paid on account of the marriage of a female person.

d) It is paid for a marriage that is intended or has taken place.

10. Person to Whom Bride-Price Is Payable

Under customary law, a father is the right person legally entitled to receive the bride-price paid in respect of his daughter in patrilineal societies in Nigeria. Where the bride's father is dead, this right is given to the male head of the immediate family. Where there is neither a father nor his successor, the girl's guardian becomes entitled to receive the bride-price.

On the other hand, where the bride is from some areas of the southern part of Nigeria where matrilineal descent is practised, the girl's maternal uncles or other members of the bride's mother's family receive the bride-price.

As a general practice, the mother of the bride under customary law is not entitled to receive the bride-price.

11. Celebration of Marriage

After all the above-mentioned requirements to a customary law marriage in Nigeria have been met, the marriage itself is contracted. In most customary law systems in Nigeria, there is no marriage until the bride is led to the house of the bridegroom or his parents and formally handed over by the father or guardian of the bride to the father or representative of the groom's family. The reason is that customary law marriage is said to be a transaction between two families and not just the individuals to the marriage.

CHAPTER TWO

WHY MARRY

INTRODUCTION

Universal acceptability of the marriage institution has directly or indirectly affected the world community. This has made it imperative for people to be married. In every part of the world, Africa in particular, a man or woman is expected to be married at the attainment of puberty. With the advent of Western education that has resulted in most people pursuing their academic dreams to older ages, the age for marriage at the expense of early marriage has increased considerably amongst the people of the middle class and the upper class.

Despite the above-mentioned, in every society, cutting across all class segments, race, religion, or culture, most people, no matter how rich or educated, do not feel fulfilled if they do not get married at least once in their lifetime. Not being married at all in one's lifetime is usually perceived as a taboo or stigma. Conceiving marriage as an imperative, to my mind, is not just a societal issue but also religious. And the Lord God said, "It is not good that the man should be alone;

I will make him an help meet for him" (Genesis 2:18). After creation, God himself saw the void in man without a companion; so he created the woman out of the man. This does not mean that there is no group of persons who genuinely remain unmarried.

> And the king spake unto Ashpenaz the master of his eunuchs, that he should bring certain of the children of Israel, and the king's seed, and of the princes; children in whom was no blemish. (Daniel 1:3-4)

> On the seventh day, when King Xerxes was in high spirits from wine, he commanded the seven eunuchs who served him. (Esther 1:10) thus saith the Lord unto the eunuchs that kept my sabbaths and choose the things that please me, and take hold of my covenant; even unto them will I give in mine house and within my walls a place and a name better than of sons and daughters; I will give them an everlasting name, that shall not be cut off. (Isaiah 56:4-5)

In our contemporary society, in the orthodox Roman Catholic Church, it is widely known that there are those who either voluntarily or by calling have decided to take the oath of chastity to remain unmarried throughout their lifetime. There are also those in either the Christian faith or other religious sects or organisations who have kept to the practice of celibacy.

May it be noted at this point that the state of being married or unmarried is a thing of choice by an individual provided the effect of the choice is not inimical to the society in general. However, more important are the reasons why people get married. What are these reasons? Are they right or wrong? What are the effects of these reasons on marriages if contracted? These are, to my mind, issues that should be looked into if the world must have good families (as intended by God) that reflect through a peaceful, loving, and caring world.

REASONS FOR GETTING MARRIED

There are several and varying reasons why people get married. It has been observed through counselling and research that various people have various reasons for getting married, though some are more commonly found across different categories of persons no matter the age, race, religion, or social status. Now let us look at some of these reasons since it is almost impossible to exhaust this list in only this book.

1. Freedom from Parents

Some believe that at a particular age in life, they need to be freed from the clutches of their parents. Nobody should truly be tied to the apron strings of a parent(s) for life, but this should not be a reason for getting married. A man or woman who is a full adult should know when he or she is ready for marriage. You may wonder why I used the word "full" to describe the word "adult". I am of the certainty of the opinion that marriage is not for children but for those who are fully ready for it mentally, emotionally, psychologically, spiritually, socially, and economically. If a man whom God from creation has positioned as the head of his family enters into marriage simply because he wants to prove to his parents that he no longer wants to remain grasped in their hands, then he is not fully mature to be called an adult, notwithstanding his age, except he understands why he needs a wife as a companion and friend to pilot the affairs of life together as one.

The same applies to a woman who intends to become a wife only because she thinks she is being controlled by her parents simply because she is single. She definitely must understand her role to a man when he becomes her husband as a help to him. It is not enough that she is married, but most have an understanding of her responsibilities after marriage.

It therefore follows that wanting to be free from one's parents cannot be a good reason to get married.

2. Age

Do not rush to get married just because you are above a certain age or because you think your biological clock is ticking. That you are not yet married at a particular age you might have set for yourself, or you see most of your friends getting married, does not mean something is wrong with you. It does not also mean that you will have no chance of getting married in the future.

You think you are running out of time to get married? *No!* This is one very wrong reason to get into a marriage contract. Lots of people have either destroyed their destinies, endured all through life, or ran out of marriage because they made the mistake of getting into marriage based on "they are running out of time". Be patient, pray, and believe that your time of glorification will also come.

3. To Be Happy and Complete

"Marriage will make me happy and complete", most people believe. *Wrong!* It is only a myth. Marriage cannot and will never make anyone, male or female, happy or complete. Saying that marriage alone makes one happy and complete is a lie. Marriage is stressful and complicated. As a single adult, there are things you do or take decisions on without consulting a second person. This position changes automatically once you get married.

As a married person, you cannot go to certain places without the consent of your spouse. May I be more practical by stating that it is even worse for a woman. The Bible says that the man is the head of his family and the wife ought to be submissive to her husband. It therefore makes it more imperative for the husband to give his consent to most of the decisions of his wife. However, this should not be interpreted to imply that the wife is a lesser being and as such be treated like a slave. She also has her decisions to make at times.

There is actually some happiness in singlehood that should be appreciated and well utilized.

> Therefore shall a man leave his father and his mother and shall cleave unto his wife: and they shall be one flesh. (Genesis 2:24)

> He who made them at the beginning made them male and female. And said, for this cause shall a man leave father and mother and shall cleave to his wife: and they twain shall be one flesh. Wherefore they are no more twain, but one flesh. (Matthew 29:4-6)

From the above quotes, it is clear that from creation God created two individual beings: one a male, the other a female. They were both complete and unique. No wonder they complement one another but did not complete one another.

Therefore, any man or woman who enters into a marriage with the intention that he or she would be complete enters into the relationship for the wrong reason.

4. To Ease Loneliness

Marriage is not a cure for loneliness. It is for companionship. Adam was not *lonely* in the Garden of Eden but was *alone*. According to the Holy Bible, in the book of Genesis, after God created everything, the firmament, waters, seas, fishes, living creatures creeping and walking upon the earth, the herbs, trees, etc., he created man last in his image to have dominion over all created things. Adam was not lonely because he was surrounded by beauty from the flowers, trees, herbs, and the animals around him. I could imagine that he was a very busy person, naming all created things. But he was alone. This is because everything created at the time was created as male and female except Adam, who had nothing similar to him. Hence, God said, "*It is not good that the man should be alone: I will make him a helpmeet for him*" (Genesis 2:18, emphasis mine).

If a spouse—a woman or man—does not feel fulfilled as a person and wants another person to fill a vacuum called loneliness in him or her, then such a person, in my opinion, will only end up being a burden to the spouse. The reason is that as long as the "disturbed" spouse cannot distinguish between being alone and being lonely, loneliness will never leave.

One can be married and still be lonely, though not alone. When a spouse decides not to communicate, show love, or relate with other members of the household and is always withdrawn, despite the fact that there are several people in the house including the wife or husband, loneliness will still be an issue. So getting married is not an antidote to loneliness.

With the improvement in technology worldwide, technology, which should ordinarily be a blessing to humanity, has become a vice in a lot of instances. Spouses now play and relate more with their computers, mobile phones, etc., than with their mates. That is loneliness.

5. A Pregnancy

Is it sufficient that a man gets married to a woman simply because she is pregnant? I hope not to be perceived as insensitive. However, if you feel otherwise, based on my opinion, it reflects our varying characteristics and uniqueness. The world would have been monotonous without varying views about issues and life in general.

In my opinion, pregnancy should not be a base for people becoming couples. Pregnancy should not, or should never, be a basis for marriage to be instituted. Marriage should naturally ensue a relationship based on friendship and mutual love. If two persons get married either because the man insists on the woman being pregnant before marital rites are done, as in most recent cases, or the woman imposes pregnancy on the man to lure him into marrying her, what then is the foundation of the marriage? What becomes of the marriage where the pregnancy terminates after the marriage? What becomes the fate of the relationship if the child dies during or shortly after birth? Or what happens when the child or children are grown and leave to their various homes. These are questions that need answers before pregnancy is used as a basis for marriage.

6. Social Pressure

This could be influenced by friends, society, and even from your psyche. In our society, pressure is often mounted on people when they are over thirty years of age. Lots of questions are asked as to why a person is not, or cannot, be married. This comes from every angle: friends, family, and society in general. This could lead to one being pressured into getting involved in a relationship which he or she may not appreciate or value in the long run. It then becomes a source of pain, regret, and frustration to the other party.

7. Gratifying Sexual Desires

This has become a major reason why most young people get married, especially in churches. It is a problem in most religious places of worship where young men and women are driven into marriage in order to satisfy their sexual desires because of the Bible's stand that fornication is a sin. Apostle Paul in the book of Corinthians wrote, "Nevertheless, to avoid fornication, let every man have his own wife and let every woman have her own husband" (1 Corinthians 7:2).

For a society to be sanitized, it ordinarily follows that every man should have his wife and every woman her own husband. Unfortunately, this has not been the case. But the question is, should people get married in order to avoid fornication? Then what happens when a spouse is unavoidably absent for months or no longer have sexual interest or ability after the marriage has been consummated?

When sex is a major reason for getting married, then such a marriage might become problematic. For instance, when a partner cannot carry out his or her sexual duties due to ill health. Also, if a man gets married because he wants to have sex, when the wife of such a man is pregnant and cannot have sexual intercourse at a particular stage of her pregnancy (like some women experience), there is every tendency that the man will become unfaithful to his spouse. This act of unfaithfulness if not properly handled or stopped could lead to divorce. The desire for sex especially amongst Christians should not be a major reason for getting married.

8. Love

Love is the most common reason people give for getting married. Love should be the major or one of the major reasons for two people getting married. Lust or infatuation has often been mistaken for love. Real love endures all things; it is not jealous, boastful, hateful, or envious. A lot of people give various reasons for falling in love. Some may be physically attracted to one another, while some others may fall in love because they belong to the same religious sects. Those who fall in love based on their faith do so because, according to the Holy Bible, they do not want to be "unequally yoked" to someone of a different religious belief. There are still a different category of people who fall in love with one another because they have similarities in their backgrounds or upbringing. This can sometimes be a strong reason why people get married. If either of these is the reason some couples get married, it should be genuine and not because they are compelled to do so. Whatever the reason for falling in love would be, however, love is one major reason why people get married.

9. Finance

Finance has played a major role as a reason for people getting married. People, especially some women, get married because they want someone to meet their financial needs. Unfortunately, in recent times, it has been known that even women who have well-paid jobs and are economically buoyant still go after men who are very rich to marry them only because of the money.

This is very common in the entertainment industry, particularly in the so-called civilized nations of the world. These women, or men in some cases, get married with the intention of divorcing and taking over part of the wealth of their spouses. Materialism and covetousness are the only things that can demean a grown person to act in such a manner. There are also those who are not financially buoyant either on their own or their parents. This makes such people, especially women, get married to men whom they would not have wanted as husbands just to gratify their financial need.

Women in this category believe that marrying men who are economically buoyant would support them and their extended family members financially. This is a common practice in most developing nations particularly in some regions in Africa. There are women whose parents might not be able to sponsor them to attain their dreams academically, and as such, get married to men who can sponsor them through school (especially when such ladies have completed their secondary education but could not go further to the university).

Some other women also get married to rich men to sponsor their siblings in their academic pursuit or even set up some businesses for them. By doing so, the status of such families change from being low in the society to becoming rich.

It should be noted that, there are men who also get married to women who are economically buoyant to finance their academic pursuit or even set up some businesses for them, hence, enabling such men to become recognised in society.

10. Sympathy

Some get married because they feel sorry for a certain man or woman due to one reason or the other. For instance, a man or woman gets married because the intended spouse is physically challenged and does not have any other person willing to marry him or her despite the person's beauty, education, or social status. Also, there are those who marry due to sympathy because of rejection that the intended spouse had faced from friends or relatives.

11. Immigration Purposes

This is a common trend all over the world, especially in the civilized world. Most people from nations whose economy is not encouraging their youths to become what they have dreamt of becoming end up in foreign countries where they get into "Green Card" marriages.

It has also been observed that there are those who have not had the privilege of travelling abroad but find women or men from their native countries who are citizens of countries in the civilized world. So they get married to them just to enable them to travel out of their native, economically unfriendly countries. Such marriages suffer tremendous challenges a lot of the time.

12. Companionship

Companion, inter alia, is "a mate: one of a pair". While companionship is the "the state of being a companion: fellowship; association". As was stated earlier, from creation, God saw Adam (though not lonely but alone) and decided to create a helpmeet for him as a companion. It is not an unknown fact that every man or woman at a certain stage in life needs a person of the opposite sex with whom to share the innermost part of his or her life no matter the success of that person in life. It is a natural thing even though some with a different school of thought like the advocates of the gay community might think otherwise, and are entitled to their opinion. But this is true.

It is even more interesting to note that, even those who are celebrities and very rich as a consequence have friends from the opposite sex whom they confide in, even when they do not engage in sexual intimacy in the relationship. Money or fame cannot replace companionship.

Companionship is, therefore, one major reason for people getting married. As I said earlier, the reasons why people get married are numerous and cannot be exhausted in this single book. Whatever might be one's reason for getting married, they should be good enough to make one embark on a lifetime journey. Marriage is what anyone entering into it, should be careful to tread on. One must be able to evaluate the reasons and weigh them with subsequent consequences if these are trifled with.

Marriage is not a game of chess. Please do not play with it; it is a bed of roses with a lot of thorns. Tread with care into it.

CHAPTER THREE

THE MONSTER

"Monster" is defined as, inter alia, "a person who is horrifyingly cruel, brutal, selfish etc. Something of extraordinarily great size". A monster from the above definition is a person who is unkind, cruel, brutal, or selfish. In my opinion, it is only someone with such terrifying qualities that can ordinarily treat his or her fellow human being (a spouse) to the point of having a marriage dissolve. Divorce itself is a monster. Yes, it is. It is hideous and abnormal in structure or appearance. It is peripheral and deceitful. It should not be a way of life, but man chose it. God said, "For this cause shall a man leave father and mother and shall cleave to his wife: and they twain shall be one flesh. Wherefore they are no more twain, but one flesh. What therefore God hath joined together, let no man put asunder" (Matthew 19:6).

He created all things, and he created man in his own image. He knew the best for the man whom he created. It was never

God's intention that what he created himself should suffer, hence the caveat. Man was stopped from the inception of the institution of marriage in the Garden of Eden between Adam and Eve from putting asunder what he has brought together. Adam named Eve woman because she was and is the flesh of his flesh and bone of his bones. That is how inseparable they are. The man-created monster called divorce should never be taken for granted and played with like kids do with toys. No! Divorce is not a toy. It is deadly, a monster, hideous and abnormal in structure and appearance.

Divorce is "the legal separation of man and wife, effected by the judgement or decree of a court, and either totally dissolving the marriage relation, or suspending its effects so far as concerns the cohabitation of the parties". It also means to repudiate one's wife or husband. Divorce could be total or partial. This means that a court of law can give a judgement ordering a divorce from the bond of marriage. A total and absolute divorce of husband and wife, dissolving the marriage tie and releasing the parties wholly from their matrimonial obligations is known as *divorce a vinculo matrimonii.*

Divorce in every society in the world has never been received by applause. Even where such is done for one reason or the other, the consequences outlive the applause. The issue of divorce shall be discussed in this book, as under the statutory law marriage and briefly under the customary law marriage system in Nigeria. It would be discussed in relation to the Christian religion.

Divorce a mensa et thoro is known as a divorce from table and bed or from bed and board. It is a partial divorce by which the parties are separated and forbidden by a court of law to live or cohabit together without affecting the marriage itself.

The intention of this book is not to make its reader go through a law class on divorce but to delve into certain issues that could cause the dissolution of a marriage. Every law made by man originated from God no matter the religion, society, or man that makes the law. It is either enacted according to how God intends it to be from creation or it is man-made, contrary to God's ways.

The divine ideal for marriage is certainly a lifelong bond that unites husband and wife in a "one flesh" relationship. The marriage union is a holy condition founded by God, and it is not to be dissolved at the will of human beings. Separation of this bond displeases God and poses a serious threat to the social order of any society. "And let none deal treacherously with the wife of his youth. For the Lord God of Israel says that He hates divorce, for it covers one's garments with violence" (Malachi 3:15).

The Law of Moses allowed a man to divorce his wife when she found "no favour in his eyes because he has found some uncleanness in her" (Deuteronomy 24:1). The primary purpose of this legislation or law was to prevent him from taking back his wife after she had married another man which was an abomination before the Lord. The law was intended to discourage divorce rather than encourage divorce. A public document known as a certificate of divorce or writing of divorcement was granted to the woman. This permitted her the right to remarry without civil or religious sanction. Divorce could not be done privately.

The Mosaic law called for severe penalties for certain types of "uncleanness". Adultery carried the death penalty by stoning for the woman. If a man believed that his wife was not a virgin when he married her, he could have her judged by the elders of the city; if they found her guilty, she could be put to death (Deuteronomy 22:13-21). This was not the case with a man. A wife was not allowed to divorce her husband for any reason. Legally, the wife was bound to her husband as long as they both lived or until he divorced her (1 Corinthians 7:39, Deuteronomy 29:1-2).

In Jesus's days, confusion prevailed about the grounds for divorce. The Pharisees (who loved being called rabbis) tempted him on this issue. There are also some Christian religious scholars who have stated that even rabbis could not agree on what constituted the "uncleanness" of Deuteronomy 24:1 of the Holy Bible.

However, followers of Rabbi Shammai felt adultery was the only ground for divorce. While those who followed Rabbi Hillel accepted many reasons including such things as poor cooking.

The Gospels record four statements by Jesus concerning divorce. In two of these, he allowed divorce in the case of adultery. (1) Jesus commented on the situation of both the woman and her new husband, "Whosoever divorces his wife for any reason except sexual immorality causes her to commit adultery; and whosoever marries a woman who is divorced commits adultery" (Matthew 5:32). (2) Jesus describes the position of the man who divorced his wife, "Whoever divorces his wife except for sexual immorality and marries another, commits adultery; and whoever marries her who is divorced commits adultery" (Matthew 19:9). While these two statements seem to allow divorce because of unfaithfulness, two other statements of Jesus in Mark 10:11-12 and Luke 16:18 respectively appear to make no provision for divorce. (3) "And He saith unto them, Whosoever shall put away his wife, and marry another, committed adultery against her. And if a woman shall put away her husband, and be married to another, she committed adultery" (Mark 10:11-12). (4) "Whosoever putteth away his wife, and marrieth another, committed adultery: and whosoever marrieth her that is put away from her husband committed adultery" (Luke 16:18).

The ultimate question then is, are Jesus' statements allowing divorce for infidelity in conflict with biblical statements that seem to forbid it entirely? Jesus' statements in Mark and Luke were made in conversations or dialogues with the Pharisees about the Mosaic law, which they believed allowed divorce on grounds other than adultery as in Deuteronomy 24:1-4, "When a man hath taken a wife and marrieth her, and it come to pass that she finds no favour in his eyes, because he had found some uncleanness in her: then let him write a bill of divorcement, and give it in her hand, and send her out of his house. And when she is departeth out of his house, she may go and be another man's wife. And if the latter husband hate her, and write her a bill of divorcement, and giveth it in her hand, and sendeth her out of his house; or if the latter husband die which took her to be a wife; Her former husband, which sent her away, may not take her again to be his wife, after that she is defiled; for that is abomination before the Lord: And thou shalt not cause the land to sin, which the Lord thy God giveth thee for an inheritance". Jesus' main point in these statements was that divorce is contrary to God's plan for marriage and should never be taken lightly. Despite the fact that Moses allowed divorce, this was an exception granted under the law because of their "hardness" of heart. Jesus desired to put "teeth" into the law by declaring that even if a divorced couple had not been sexually unfaithful to one another, they would be committing adultery in God's sight if they now got married to other partners. By allowing divorce for the single reason of immorality or illicit sexual intercourse, though grievous, Jesus' thought is clearly that a person dissolves his marriage by creating a sexual union with someone other than the marriage partner. Such union is completely at variance with the sacred oneness intended by God when he united Adam and Eve in the first marriage relationship.

In the case of sexual unfaithfulness, the decree of divorce simply reflects the fact that the marriage has already been broken. A man divorcing his wife for this cause does not "make her an adulteress", for she already is one. Thus, divorce on the ground of unchastity usually frees the innocent partner to remarry without incurring the guilt of adultery. However, this is sometimes questioned. Although Jesus allowed divorce for adultery, he did not require it. On the contrary, he insisted that divorce disrupts God's plan for marriage and left the way open for repentance and forgiveness.

Paul was essentially in agreement with Jesus' teachings on marriage and divorce. However, the apostle dealt with new situations involving the marital conflict between believers and between a believer and an unbeliever.

In the case of two Christians, he admonished them to follow the Lord's teachings and be reconciled. In any event, neither is to marry another as written in 1 Corinthians 7:10-11. In 1 Corinthians 7:15, Paul wrote that a Christian whose spouse has abandoned the marriage should be free to formalize the divorce. "If the unbeliever departs, let him depart; a brother or a sister is not under bondage in such cases" (1 Corinthians 7:15). Many authorities have interpreted the phrase "not under bondage" to mean that the deserted Christian spouse may lawfully go from divorce to remarriage. But other scholars disagree with this interpretation. In any event, Paul encourages the believer to keep the marriage together in the hope that the unbelieving partner might be saved.

DIVORCE AS VIEWED BY LAW

From the foregoing, therefore, either by law as we know it in Nigeria or the Holy Bible, divorce is not an easy venture for any married couple to embark upon. In Nigeria, before the Matrimonial Causes Act, 1970, which is the overriding law guiding the statutory marriage in Nigeria, promulgated by the then military regime, the law on divorce was based on the matrimonial offence theory. This was from the fact that the law on matrimonial causes in effect in England from time to time was applicable in Nigeria. Therefore, changes in English law in this respect became part of Nigerian law.

In England, the matrimonial offence theory dates back to the old ecclesiastical courts which originally had sole jurisdiction in the dissolution of marriages. Even when in 1857 the secular divorce was introduced, the matrimonial offence theory was introduced, the matrimonial offence theory continued to hold sway. By this theory, a marriage may only be dissolved when a spouse commits any of these matrimonial offences like adultery, discretion, or cruelty.

The move from the matrimonial offence principle in some parts of the commonwealth dates back to 1920 when the New Zealand legislature began to experiment with the principle of breakdown of marriage. In England, however, the new trend gathered weight and acceptability with the appointment by the

Archbishop of Canterbury in January of 1964 a group to review the law of England concerning divorce.

The group in 1966 recommended inter alia in its report a complete change of the English law of divorce by abandoning the offence theory and adopting the breakdown of marriage principle as the basis of divorce law. Following the report by the review group, the then lord high chancellor of Great Britain referred the report to the law commission for advice. In its report, the "Reform on the Grounds of Divorce: The Field of Choice", the commission put forward a compromise solution which, while admitting the introduction of breakdown as a basis for divorce, retained the old matrimonial offence principle. The report formed the basis of the amending legislation of the 1969 Divorce Reform Act, of which Nigeria benefited immensely.

By the provisions of the Matrimonial Causes Act, 1970, of Nigeria, either party to a marriage may petition for divorce "upon the ground that the marriage has broken down irretrievably". Note that the word "ground" (singular) rather than "grounds" (plural) was stated in the act. This should not in any way confuse any reader. The act went further to subdivide the ground into grounds under which a marriage may be said to have broken-down irretrievably if proven by a petitioner. Moreover, it has been decided by a court of appeal in Nigeria in the case of *Ezirim v. Ezirim* that under the 1970 Matrimonial Causes Act, for a petitioner to be able to establish irretrievable breakdown of a marriage as a sole ground. "It is necessary to bear in mind the fact that although the Act (Matrimonial Causes Act) created only one ground of divorce, to wit, that the marriage has irretrievably broken down, yet that the facts which may lead to the marriage breaking down irretrievably are categorized under sub-sections (a) to (h) of section 15(2). Only those facts can suffice to found a petition for divorce. In other words, a court hearing a petition for divorce ought not to hold that the marriage has irretrievably broken down unless the petitioner or cross-petitioner, as the case may be, satisfies the court on one or more of the…facts".

It must be noted that *the first objective of a divorce law is to ensure that divorce is not so easy as to dissuade the parties from making efforts to overcome their matrimonial difficulties.* The provisions under the Matrimonial Causes Act, 1970, which makes the proof of one or more of the following enable the courts, determine that a marriage has broken down irretrievably is meant to protect the marriage institution and prevent couples to run down to a court of law for every trivial misunderstanding between them. The above mentioned provisions are as follows:

Grounds for dissolution of marriage

(1) A petition under this Act by a party to a marriage for a decree of dissolution of the marriage may be presented to the court by either party to the marriage upon the ground that the marriage has broken down irretrievably.

(2) The court hearing a petition for a decree of dissolution of a marriage shall hold the marriage to have broken down irretrievably if, but only if, the petitioner satisfies the court of one or more of the following facts-

    (a) that the respondent has willfully and persistently refused to consummate the marriage;

    (b) that since the marriage the respondent has committed adultery and the petitioner finds it intolerable to live with the respondent;

(c) that since the marriage the respondent has behaved in such a way that the petitioner cannot reasonably be expected to live with the respondent;

(d) that the respondent has deserted the petitioner for a continuous period of at least one year immediately preceding the presentation of the petition;

(e) that the parties to the marriage have lived apart for a continuous period of at least two years immediately preceding the presentation of the petition and the respondent does not object to a decree being granted;

(f) that the parties to the marriage have lived apart for a continuous period of a least three years immediately preceding the presentation of the petition;

(g) that the other party to the marriage has, for a period of not less than one year, failed to comply with a decree or restitution of conjugal rights made under his Act;

(h) that the other party to the marriage has been absent from the petitioner for such time and in such circumstances as to provide reasonable grounds for presuming that he or she is dead.

(3) For the purposes of subsection (2) (e) and (f) of this section the parties to a marriage shall be treated as living apart unless they are living with each other in the same household.

16. Provisions supplementary to section 15

(1) Without prejudice to the generality of section 15 (2) of this Act, the court hearing a petition for a decree of dissolution of marriage shall hold that the petitioner has satisfied the court of the fact mentioned in the

said section 15 (2) (c) of this Act if the petitioner satisfies the court that-

(a) since the marriage, the respondent has committed rape, sodomy, or bestiality; or

(b) since the marriage, the respondent has, for a period of not less than two years-

    (i) been a habitual drunkard; or

    (ii) habitually been intoxicated by reason of taking or using to excess any sedative, narcotic or stimulating drug or preparation, or has, for a part or parts of such a period, been a habitual drunkard and has, for the other part or parts of the period, habitually been so intoxicated; or

(c) since the marriage, the respondent has within a period not exceeding five years-

    (i) suffered frequent convictions for crime in respect of which the respondent has been sentenced in the aggregate to imprisonment for not less than three years; and

    (ii) habitually left the petitioner without reasonable means of support; or

(d) since the marriage, the respondent has been in prison for a period of not less than three years after conviction for an offence punishable by death or imprisonment for life or for a period of five years or more, and is still in prison at the date of the petition; or

(e) since the marriage and within a period of one year immediately preceding the date of the petition, the respondent has been convicted of-

    (i) having attempted to murder or unlawfully to kill the petitioner; or

(ii) having committed an offence involving the intentional infliction of grievous harm or grievous hurt on the petitioner or the intent to inflict grievous harm or grievous hurt on the petitioner; or

(f) the respondent has habitually and willfully failed, throughout the period of two years immediately preceding the date of the petition, to pay maintenance for the petitioner-

(i) ordered to be paid under an order of, or an order registered in, a court in the Federation; or

(ii) agreed to be paid under an agreement between the parties to the marriage providing for their separation; or

(g) the respondent-

(i) is, at the date of the petition, of unsound mind and unlikely to recover; and

(ii) since the marriage and within the period of six years immediately preceding the date of the petition, has been confined for a period of, or for periods aggregating, not less than five years in an institution where persons may be confined for unsoundness of mind in accordance with law, or in more than one such institution.

(2) Where a petition is based on the fact mentioned in section 15 (2) (h) of this Act-

(a) proof that, for a period of seven years immediately preceding the date of the petition, the other party to the marriage was continually absent from the petitioner and that the petitioner has no reason to believe that the other party was alive at any time within that period, is sufficient to establish the fact in question, unless it is shown that the other party to the marriage was alive at a time within that period; and

(b) a decree made pursuant to the petition shall be in the form of a decree of dis- solution of marriage by reason of presumption of death.

The law of divorce in Nigeria makes *divorce proceedings cumbersome*, thus discouraging divorce in our society. This does not imply that when indeed there is merit in the claims of a petitioner, that divorce may not be granted. The law protects the marriage institution which, when it breaks down, affects not only the parties to the marriage but also the children and the larger society. It is cancerous and eats deep down into the entire fabrics of a society.

One must not lose focus of the fact that this monster is not peculiar to Nigeria. It exists in other nations of the world, particularly the developed nations such as the United States of America (USA), Canada, and Europe. It is rather pathetic to observe that in these parts of the world, particularly the USA, couples get married and divorced almost as regularly as marriages are transacted. The law, especially in some states, allows divorce even in a few days after the marriage vow. This is so common especially amongst celebrities. Marriage is not a game, and divorce is not a toy and should never be played with. The consequences of divorce in most cases are for life. It can destroy or dent the future or image of the parties to the marriage and leave a scar on the individuals and their offspring where children are involved. It leaves bitterness, disillusionment, and pain in the hearts of the parties, children, other family members, and friends. It goes beyond the two individuals directly involved.

For a better and greater Nigeria and world, for a greater, happier, more peaceful, and more successful future for our children, youths, and even those unborn, let us all join our hands to say no to this monster, once it is sensed creeping into our homes. We can! Yes, we can!

On the issue of divorce with the customary law marriage system, the procedure varies from one custom or community to another as discussed in chapter one. There is no uniform principle guiding this system. Return of the bride-price, however, cuts across almost all communities.

STATUTORY MARRIAGE VIS-À-VIS CUSTOMARY MARRIAGE DIVORCE

The system of marriage contracted by parties to a marriage has varying legal implications as regarding the right of the parties particularly the wife and the offspring of that marriage. A statutory marriage under the Marriage Act can only be dissolved by a court of law which does not apply to the customary law of marriage. Whatever may be the type of marriage entered into by the parties to a marriage, the effect of divorce and its consequences are the same emotionally, psychologically, and socially. The major difference may be economical, especially in countries where alimonies are paid to a spouse who is the victim of the relationship. This is more so in countries where almost every property owned by the man is given to the woman because the law sees her as the vulnerable party.

Should one then, for economic reasons alone, mortgage the future, love, peace, and joy of a spouse and children and become a menace to the society? The effects of divorce on the entire society outweigh the momentary pleasure *and* pseudo sense of freedom enjoyed by an individual.

It is not intended in this book to suggest that, no matter how unsatisfied a spouse is in a marriage, the unhappy partner should remain in the marriage. One is aware of the fact that some spouses can be very violent, which could also result in the loss of life. It is better to be alive to deal with the difficulties of divorce than to suffer death.

When a person notices his or her spouse to be violent, it is always good to seek counsel early. This assistance could be gotten from the church, other religious organisations, or professional bodies to help the violent partner. It would also enable the person violated to cope better psychologically and emotionally. But where the needed assistance does not yield the expected outcome, either because the violent partner refused to be helped or is not willing to change, the violated spouse should at least be temporarily separated from the violent party.

That notwithstanding, spouses should do all they should to avoid divorce, more so when children are involved in that marriage. Parties should know that marriage is a bed of roses with lots of thorns. Thorns are never easy to handle by anyone, but if carefully handled, it does not hurt and on the stem blossoms the sweet-smelling rose. So scents the aroma of a successful marriage in any environment that affects the society positively. Where this fails, however, I believe the party who wants the marriage to work but is deprived and frustrated is free to leave and forge on with life.

Children from intact homes most of the time, though not always, positively affect and influence their society as well as those they come in contact with.

Their positive behaviour and attitude are positively contagious which in turn produces a great and peaceful society or nation.

CHAPTER FOUR

FACTORS INHIBITING THE SUCCESS OF MARRIAGE— SOCIOLOGICAL PERSPECTIVE

It is fair to state that there is no one cause for any divorce. There are often several factors. But researchers have come up with several reasons as causes of divorce.

1. Social Tolerance

The social acceptance of divorce, rather than be seen as a taboo, is one major cause of divorce. People are no longer willing to endure petty problems and misunderstandings in marriage, and they give no thought to their marriage vows that say "for better, for worse". In fact, there are churches that preach that such phrases as "for better, for worse" are unscriptural, thereby resulting in some of their faithfuls who do not apply wisdom to their understanding, quitting their marriage with the slightest provocation by a spouse. Indeed, remarriage is encouraged once the first marriage is dissolved in some instances.

The church is a place of refuge and good counsel through the power of the Holy Spirit. The body of Christ should stand by the tenets of the teachings of the Lord Jesus Christ and endeavour to see that if divorce is on the increase in the secular world, the church should serve as a good example, rather than going the way of the world so much in need of counsel from God's people. The monster divorce is an indication of hardness of heart. Marriage from its origin was meant for life. Man changed this God-given gift by treating the wife or husband (as the case may be) of one's youth treacherously. Its consequences are disastrous, and every hand ought to be on deck to fight this enemy of the twenty-first century as a deadly disease to humanity.

2. Communication

If you think of a ship and its crew or a sporting team and its players, you will understand how important it is to communicate with everyone involved. Things need to happen when sailing, and commands must be clear, timely, and acted upon. In a game of football, it is essential that players on the same team communicate with one another in order to run their play. The way to win in all these examples is to communicate properly and do so whenever it is necessary. Ambiguity should be avoided. Presumptive approach should not be put up in the home and relationship. If there is a problem, trying the silent routine or the "bury your head in the sand" response is a most likely sign of heading for a divorce. Spouses should endeavour to have good communication in their relationships.

3. Commitment

A marriage is a partnership, and it takes two people to make it work. If both partners do not care about the relationship, then their marriage will certainly end in divorce. Even if only one partner does not commit wholeheartedly to the marriage, the marriage can still be undone. Both partners need to be committed, and it almost always means making sacrifices, which is what commitment is all about. Without solid support for the partnership from both parties, their families, and friends, divorce could very well be a possibility.

4. Money—Low Income or No Income

Many married couples face the challenge of money shortage which, if not properly and promptly handled, could be inimical to the marriage. The love for money is supposedly the cause of all evil, and it definitely is the cause of arguments, fights, and court actions in some instances. One spouse spends money without telling the other partner. One spouse loses a job and the combined income falls and certain needs of the family can no longer be met. The problem boils down to money or having none at all.

There is a school of thought that believes that couples who are relatively successful with their finances are less likely to argue and thus head towards divorce. This, in my opinion, varies from one marriage to another and the persons involved in the marriages. Financial success, per se, cannot reduce the rate of divorce in a society. Their attitude towards one another and their financial success is more of a factor for the success of the marriage than the finances. There are a lot of marriages that end in divorce, especially in Nigeria, when one party, particularly the man, becomes prosperous. His new status makes him believe he also needs a new life. This leads to divorce.

Knowing the importance of money in any human existence, emphasis should be placed at this point on this very necessary but sometimes very destructive element called money. I said earlier that no income or low income is a factor that is responsible for divorce in some marriages. Money, of course, is very important to any marriage.

I have personally seen cases and even heard from others or through my counselling session with some clients who told me how a man will walk up to a woman and propose to her, asking her hand in marriage. Do you know that neither this man nor his intended wife has a job or a means of livelihood but they believe that God will use other people to bless them? Yes, there is nothing wrong with exercising your faith in God, but do not forget that it is the same God that says he has given you the power to make wealth.

Why should any right-thinking person be planning his marriage without a dime either in his pocket or bank account? And why should a woman (his intended wife) accept such a proposal? Did God not create Adam and instruct him to dress the Garden of Eden before creating Eve as a wife and helpmeet for him? Please let us stop taking this thing too far. This problem is actually being perpetrated in our society by some so-called Christians. God does not and will never encourage laziness or idleness. Rather, it is God's will that his children prosper. "Beloved, I wish above all things that thou mayest prosper and be in health, even as thy soul prospereth" (3 John 2).

I believe with all certainty that people should get married with some financial preparation to be able to carry out some of their responsibilities. Definitely, no man can have everything before going into marriage or else he will stop working for life from the day he gets married. No man should go into marriage without at least being sure of a regular source of income for his intended wife, himself, and the children that will be born later. If the man, for any reason, does not have a source of regular income at the time of the marriage, the wife-to-be should be in a position to sustain the family pending when he is gainfully employed or has a regular source of income. This should be discussed before embarking on any marriage. After all, God says that a man who is unable to fend for his household is worse than an infidel.

It is really surprising to note that some of the Christian men who fall victim to getting married without any source of regular income are encouraged to do so by other Christians. How dare you disturb a young man who may not have a good education or job, or a man who already has a good education but without any means of income, on when he would be getting married? Why not ask him and, if possible, assist him on how to sustain himself on a regular basis first, rather than assisting him to get married and subsequently make a beggar of him? Such couples have lost their self-respect in most cases, suffered low self-esteem, which can even result in a divorce when a partner can no longer cope with the shame and embarrassment of living in poverty or wallowing in poverty. This trend of disturbing penniless and jobless people to marry should be discouraged within the Christian community.

As children of God, we are not expected to be poor. It is his will for his people to have an all-round prosperity. We are expected to prosper spiritually, in health, and materially. Anything contrary to that is not the best for any child of God. But this does not mean wealth should be gotten at all cost even when it is against God's way. There are laid-down principles of God's way of acquiring wealth in his Word. People should follow his ways and leave the rest for him. No matter the situation, if you believe and work, he always makes a way.

I do not think that anyone can be blamed if a spouse in a marriage as described above calls it a quit. To my mind, a couple of that sort never had an understanding of what marriage is intended to be from the onset and should never have been married at all.

I also will never subscribe to a woman or man to remain in a very violent marriage where he or she might die prematurely. They should seek counsel early enough to avoid a divorce if possible.

5. Wrong Expectation

Children can suffer greatly from their parents having wrong expectations. They are promised a treat. It could be a visit, an outing, or present, but the parent is unable to fulfill the same. Expectations are dashed. The same can be true of some marriages. One partner wants to think for the other spouse and wants to live happily ever after. The other partner also has a life to live and think for himself or herself. We are all human; we all have faults. Do not see your partner as the perfect person. Be prepared to discover, accept, and tolerate faults which you either did not know about or thought would never cause a problem. Be hopeful and confident, but do not allow your expectations to reach heights which may never be realized. This could be frustrating and devastating. If expectations are repeatedly dashed, there is the tendency of the hurt party believing he or she is not loved by the other spouse. This could result in a divorce.

6. Midlife Crisis

The exact definition of this phenomenon varies from person to person, but in men, it usually means a desire to change job, location, or lifestyle. They think their life is getting to a stage where they need a new challenge. In Nigeria, it could even be the acceptance of chieftaincy titles, which at times is accompanied with a new wife or wives, as the case may be.

It is possible that they may, but such abrupt and seemingly selfish determination can have a big impact on their spouses. Massive change may be scary or unnecessary to the spouse. The turmoil from this new lust for life can be the cause of many divorces among couples who have been married for several years.

7. Little Things

It seems hard to believe things such as a partner's habit of snoring is the cause of certain marriage failures, but it may be true, at least in part. Not being able to get enough sleep every night can be enormously stressful, but you would think a loving spouse will find another bed or bedroom or seek professional help for the partner. However, if a marriage is already under strain for other reasons such as money troubles, a small thing like snoring could be the straw to break the camel's back.

8. Childlessness

The inability of couples to give birth to children due to barrenness or impotency is one major cause of divorce in developing countries such as Nigeria as well as other nations. Childlessness, in most African nations, is perceived as a taboo since it is believed that it could result in the extinction of a family. It is most pathetic to note still that there are communities in Nigeria where even when the couple has children but no male child, the marriage is seen as a failure since it is believed that the absence of a male child means the end of the family lineage. Female children in such communities are treated more like second-class citizens in their fathers' houses. Childlessness is one of the most common causes of divorce because the absence of children leads to loneliness and weariness, they claim. The placement of a girl child as no child where a male child or children are not born by couples is an unfair treatment and a violation of the fundamental human right of such individuals. Before the eyes of God and the law, everyone is equal and should be so respected.

9. Interference by Third Parties

a) Extended Family Members

The extended family system, which encourages members of extended family such as fathers, mothers, uncles, aunties, etc., to partake in some decision-making processes in a nuclear family, is a commonly found reason for failed marriages in Nigeria. Partners, especially men, allow their relations to decide what happens in their homes. By doing so, they give undue powers to such relations who most of the time come with the aim of destroying rather than building up marriages.

b) Unfriendly Friends

The dictionary meaning of a friend is one who cherishes kind regard for another person, an intimate and trustworthy companion. On the contrary, there are those who pretend to be friends while in reality they are envious and negatively competitive. They always wished they drove the car you drive, wore the clothes you wear, lived in the type of house you live in, married the wife or husband you are married to. Beware! Those are not true friends but "unfriendly friends" who appear to be friends on the outside but within they seek your downfall.

They come in sheep's clothing to give counsel when there is a problem in the marriage, but deep down, they pray that your marriage that gives you joy and happiness and your spouse that makes you feel "thick" depart from you so you can become like them, or even worse. They are indeed wolves in sheep's clothing. Many have become victims of such "friends" and have ended their marriages, which they never intended to, and some lose their lives due to frustration, depression or unhappiness. While the "friends" mock them from a distance and in some instances, pretend to mourn with them.

10. Lack of Respect

Mutual respect for one another in a marriage partnership is one main key to an enduring and successful marriage. It has been observed, and rightly too, that there are spouses who lack respect for one another or a spouse who displays so much disrespect for his or her partner. It can be so terrible that the man, in most cases, would show a high degree of disrespect to his wife before his relations, friends, former and present girlfriends, colleagues, and even before his employees as well as domestic servants.

This lack of respect is portrayed in the form of physical assault through violence, abusive words, instructing domestic servants such as drivers to disallow their wives from using either his or the family cars which he may have bought with his money, etc. Ever wondered why any responsible man would want to be in comfort while taking pleasure in seeing his wife (who is bone of his bones and flesh of his flesh) suffer or be abused? Where lies the admonition from the Holy Scriptures that so ought men to love their wives as their own bodies and that he that loves his wife loves himself (Ephesians 5:28)? It is absurd for a man who once said "I love you" to a woman to turn around and treat her with so much contempt and disrespect after marrying her.

Women also show disrespect by nagging their husbands. Worse still are those who may be in better-paid jobs or businesses and earn higher incomes. Also, lacking in respect are wives who have house-husbands either because the latter have lost their jobs or are unemployed.

Marriage is a partnership in which if one is weak, the stronger partner ought to be a support to the other rather than being a terror. Two joined together by God are better than one because they have a good reward for their labour.

11. Dissimilarity of Background

Research has shown that where there is a wide disparity in religious, social, educational, and economic background of a couple, it could pose some problems. This could range from their ideas about life in general, their perception of things, the things they do in terms of activities in the form of occupation or leisure, types of food they eat, clothes they wear, and places they visit.

If one spouse, particularly the wife, is from a background that is more socially, educationally, and economically prominent as opposed to that of the husband, her actions could easily be misunderstood and misinterpreted by the husband, extended family members or friends. This is more so if the man is easily influenced by members of his extended family. That could result in divorce. Different religious beliefs may also cause divorce if they are not handled with utmost care.

12. Wrong Spiritual Foundations in Families and Communities

It has been observed that there are some families and communities who, through their history, have lineages where divorce is a common end to a marriage. This, some believe, might not be mere coincidence but is as a result of one's spiritual foundations. There are indeed some families where their women cannot remain in their husbands' homes, as such, do not understand why any woman married to their brothers or male relatives should have successful marriages. Women from such families will do everything possible to destroy the marriages of their male relatives.

In fact, they see spouses having successful marriages as abnormal or a taboo. Some would even go to the extent of encouraging their brothers to be unfaithful to their wives as well as have children outside the marriage. These women also believe that it is a taboo for a man from such a family or community to have all his children born by one wife.

Where several families from a community believe in such obnoxious practice, marriages are bound to be destroyed. This inhuman behavioural pattern is carried out daily in some communities around the world, thereby destroying a lot of marriages. This evil belief is so strong in some African communities, especially in some parts of Nigeria, that it will only take the intervention of God to pull these communities out of their wrong belief system.

13. Early Marriage

Early marriage is another cause of divorce in most nations of the world. The trend of immature people getting married has a negative effect on society. The question is, who is an immature person? An immature person is simply one who is not mature, fully grown, or developed. Merely attaining the constitutional or legally acceptable age of maturity, which is eighteen (18), does not necessarily make one developed enough for marriage.

Some of these negative effects are stopping school abruptly. This can result in some of the affected young ladies not continuing their education and in return not able to contribute meaningfully to society. There is also the effect of these women not being able to impart knowledge adequately to their children when born.

Another negative effect of early marriage on the larger society is premature death that could occur during childbirth. Such death could sometimes arise from the underdevelopment of the reproductive system of the very young women given out in marriage. There is also a high level of infant mortality of babies born by these mothers.

The issue of inadequate finances where some fathers are unable to provide for their families is also prevalent. This is because women who are given out in marriage at a very young age with little or no education cannot have well paying jobs to support their families.

Again, the alarming number of widows in Africa could be attributed to early marriage. Some of these widows are quite young while their deceased husbands are much older. These widows, if married, their children where applicable, are usually maltreated by relations of such deceased husbands in most cases. Indeed, they suffer what I refer to as a cycle of ill-fate. Early marriage therefore should never be encouraged in any society.

Unfortunately, especially in the so-called developed nations of the world where children are either forced or made to leave their parents' homes once they turn eighteen years of age, they automatically assume they are also mature for marriage and as such get married. This, in my opinion, is an abuse of marriage because they hardly understand what it entails to be married. Such people end up being married several times during their lifetime.

Marriages are still arranged in many parts of the world by parents in order to enhance family resources, reputation, and alliances because such parents feel more qualified to choose partners for their children. In Africa, parents, especially in rural settlements, take delight in ensuring that their children are married to people from either their own communities or from the same ethnic group. It could be said then that this idea is the major factor for parents choosing or arranging spouses for their children in these parts of the world.

It has also been observed that immigrants from the Middle East, South Asia, and some parts of Africa living in places such as Canada, America, and Europe sometimes have their marriages arranged. These may involve returning to the home country to marry a partner selected by family members still living there. Young people involved in arranged marriages on strong objection are expected to have veto power over their families' choices in some countries of the world. In some of such countries, considerable pressure exists for people to abide by the judgement of elders.

It could be said therefore, that arranged or early marriages have been one of the causes of most divorce cases or at times unhappy marriages that sooner or later results in the early death in young couples.

14. Epidemic/Pandemic

An epidemic is an outbreak of diseases that spread quickly and affect many individuals within a population, community or region at the same time.

A pandemic is also an outbreak of a disease that occurs over a wide geographic area such as multiple countries or continents. It typically affects a significant proportion of the population.

Both the pandemic and epidemic are an outbreak of a disease. The characteristic difference between the two is that, the former affects a larger geographical area such as countries, continent or the world at large. While the latter, though widespread, affects a relatively smaller proportion of the world's population and geographical area.

Examples of the two different types of outbreak of diseases are the Cholera Pandemics of several different seasons that spanned between 1824–1975. There are still occasional occurrences of outbreaks especially in communities ravaged by war or some natural disasters.

"Spanish" flu of 1918 – 19.

Severe Acute Respiratory disease Syndrome (SARS) with a first outbreak in November of 2002 before it slowly reduced, and by May 2004 no cases were being reported.

Ebola Virus Disease (EVD) was also identified for the first time in 1979 in Sudan and the Democratic Republic of the Congo at a village near the Ebola river. There were numerous outbreaks across sub-Saharan Africa.

The spread that became most deadly spread throughout West Africa and even across borders which lasted between December 2013 and January 2016.

The Coronavirus disease 2019, popularly known as COVID-19 is however the most widely experienced and infectious pandemic known to humanity. It is still on going as at present with its incessant consequences on a vast majority of the world's population.

It is not the intent of the author to delve into all the various pandemics and epidemics that had and is still affecting humanity but to mention just a few in order to discuss some of the negative effects epidemics and or pandemics could have on a marriage.

There are numerous impacts an epidemic or pandemic can have on families. These are either positive or negative.

Members of families get closer to one another during periods of pandemics. An example of such is the world-wide lockdown season of the COVID-19 pandemic. It afforded most members of the various families who ordinarily due to their busy schedule would never have been together for a long period of time, to stay together.

They cooked, had their meals together all the time, did home chores, played games or other activities together as well getting to know and understand each and every member of the family.

There were little or no contacts with people who are not members of their immediate households. This actually reduced contact between spouses who are not faithful to the other spouse in the marriage permanently, or at least temporarily cut off extra-marital sex with others apart from their wives or husbands.

On the other hand, the pandemic caused some families to lose their loved ones and in some cases, the bread winner of such families. In those situations, families suffer both emotionally and economically.

Pandemics especially during lockdown exposes the weakness (es) in each spouse which if not properly handled can subsequently cause separation or divorce of those couples.

Some people lose their source of income or livelihood during the pandemic and this can affect the families' standard of living. A country, countries or the world where applicable suffers recession during and after a pandemic which lasts for a long period of time.

Children suffer so much as well during such times. An example of that is when schools were shut down during the lockdown of COVID-19 in the 2020/2021 academic session This affected almost every child of school age all over the world emotionally and psychologically. University or college students were not exempted.

Not all children across the world had access to the internet to have visual learning platforms. Those who did, felt the absence of no interpersonal interactions with their teachers and class-mates, so learning became quite difficult for them. The educational sector all over the world suffered and may suffer for a long period of time before recovery.

A lot of people suffered and may continue to go through mental illnesses such as depression, drug addiction, anger, suicidal feeling etc as a consequence of the pandemic which can also affect the family.

In fact, every sector of the society suffers tremendously during epidemics or pandemics though the COVID-19 pandemic has been the worst ever experienced all over the world.

CHAPTER FIVE

THE TANGLED WEB OF DIVORCE

Divorce, which was a rare phenomenon before the close of the twentieth century, has apparently become commonplace today. It is being done so freely and frequently as if it has no negative effect on children and society. The prevalence of single parents in our society today, appears to have caused some negative effects on the children from such families. This is such that they are seemingly demanding the value and essence of marriage when they are neither cared for nor have a role model to copy from. Divorce has suddenly become a precipitator of moral decay and insecurity in our society.

Scholar Laha G. B. in 2007 in a paper presented in a conference in Nigeria lamented that since children have no good moral examples to copy from and no moral values are inculcated into them by some parents in a divorced family, they turned around to develop their own. The situation apparently has given rise to social vices and psychological trauma which require urgent attention.

The "web" is a snare staring us in the face in every modern society in the twenty-first century. It is as complex as the consequences. It is a conglomeration of various consequences that arise from different divorced marriages into the entire society. The solution is in keeping away from or checkmating the monster called divorce and win the game of marriage in our society.

One might wonder at this juncture what this web is all about. It is simply the tangled web of divorce also known as the consequences of divorce. The word "web" is defined among other things as "the network of *delicate* threads spun by a spider to *entrap* its *prey*; a cobweb. Any complex network: a web of highways; anything *artfully* contrived or *elaborated into a trap or snare*".

From the definition above, it is in my opinion very clear that divorce, which to the party desiring that a marriage be dissolved, might appear exciting as a web of highways that is artfully designed, which may eventually become a great trap to the parties involved. The consequences of divorce are so traumatic, though they come as various delicate threads spun to entrap its prey, that it should be avoided.

A reader might be thinking of the world wide web (www) and the Internet at this point as we talk about the web. Incidentally, this book does not intend to discuss the web and the Internet, but as earlier stated, the tangled web of divorce is what we are talking about. However, one would not lose sight of the fact that the Internet has played a major role in some broken marriages all over the world. This is because a lot of married men are hooked on the web to pornography. There are both men and women unfortunately, who are married but date others on the web.

However, the web and the Internet have their positive sides. For instance, the world has become a global village where people from different parts of the world now connect with one another very easily. Knowledge, ideas, and exchange of services within a very short space of time have increased. These are some good aspects of the web and the Internet that should be commended.

Before one goes on to discuss the consequences of divorce, it is necessary that we understand who a single parent is. There are different classes of single parents.

These are the following:

i.   widowed young mothers or fathers,
ii. Unwed mothers,
iii. Unwed fathers
iv. divorced mothers or fathers.

These different categories of single parents suffer different problems. Anyway, to enable one to understand who a single parent is, it is proper that we know the definition of a parent. A parent is "a father or mother. Any organism that generates another; a producer. Cause, occasion…parent, ancestors". On the other hand, parenthood is "the condition or relation of a parent".

A parent whether single or married, as in humans, is a father or mother. While parenthood is the condition or fact of being related or connected, or by which things are connected either objectively or in the mind.

A single parent might be a father or mother who lives with or takes care of his or her child or children without the other partner. Single parenthood does not necessarily occur because one partner is no longer alive. Both parents might still be alive but live separately, but the child resides with one of them—in most cases, with the mother (as in the case of divorced or unwed mothers). The resident parent is usually referred to as a single parent. In single parenthood, it does not matter whether the child or children are taken out on visitation or vacation by the visiting parent as long as the resident parent remains the custodian of the offspring.

With this understanding of who a single parent is, let us delve into the consequences of divorce.

CONSEQUENCES OF DIVORCE ON THE PARTIES, CHILDREN, AND SOCIETY

The effects of divorce on any society cannot be overemphasized, but they are numerous. They cannot all be discussed in a single book such as this, but I will attempt to deal with it with all seriousness of purpose that it deserves.

Many studies have concluded that children from one-parent families experience more negative outcomes than do children from two-parent families. These include lower educational attainment, behavioural problems, delinquency, leaving home earlier, and premarital pregnancy for girls and higher divorce rates when they marry. The research question typically focuses on whether negative outcomes result from the parental conflicts during marriage, the trauma of separation, the absence of a father, or some other factors. That is what I will endeavour to decipher as you read on. It is worthy of note, however, that it has been shown that mothers typically retain the custody of the children.

Despite negative media or social attention given to single-parent families, most children from these families do not experience problems, although they have a higher risk of problems than do children from two-parent families. In fact, the consequences of divorce on children and society are many, though they vary from one social class to another and from one individual to another.

Diminished Contact with Fathers

Studies have indicated that children who live with their mothers after divorce are likely to experience diminished contact with their fathers and so suffer distress from this loss. As children grow older, the time they spend with the on-resident parent decreases and about a third lose contact completely. However, father-child contact is not the deciding factor in children's adjustment after their parents separate, as frequent contact with their father may negatively impact children's well-being if there is a high amount of conflict between father and child or between parents over the children. If conflict is absent or cur-tailed, children both want and benefit from frequent contact with both parents. In general, a close relationship with both parents is associated with a positive adjustment in children after divorce. Furthermore, whether or not the father continues to pay child support may influence both the children's adjustment and the socio-economic status of the lone-parent family.

Higher Divorce Rate

Adult children of divorced parents are more likely than those from intact marriages to end their own marriages with divorce.

This may result from poor role models in childhood from the simple observation that there is life after marriage, or from the fact that divorce becomes more personally acceptable as a solution to an unhappy marriage if it has already happened in one's own family.

It is clear that parental separation adds stress to children's lives through changes in relationship, living situation, and parental resources. Although most studies found that psychological and behavioural stress is prevalent for children from separated parents, few studies concluded that psychological disturbance is severe or prolonged.

Researchers found, on the contrary, that for a very insignificant number of cases, to children from divorced parents, it is a welcome end to being witnesses to very dysfunctional relationships.

Economic Benefit

However, there are still some children who, for their own selfish reasons, prefer that the parents are divorced to enable them to benefit economically from both sides. This is commonly found among children who have parents of very high economic status. Such children think more of what they gain financially than their social and psychological well-being.

Comfort and Pleasure of Parents

It was also shown that most parents of divorced families think more of themselves than the offspring of the marriage and took that way. These are parents who consider their comfort and pleasure more than the prolonged psychological effect of divorce on their children. To children from such homes, it was observed that the realities of divorce appeared harder for them to bear than living with the marital unhappiness of their parents.

Sense of Insecurity

There is a high sense of insecurity on the part of the children and lack of trust. It is very difficult for them to trust anyone around them since they feel betrayed by those closest to them in life—that is, their parents.

Guilt/ Low Self-esteem

Some children of divorce often reason that their very existence brought about their parents' divorce. They make statements like "If I had never been born, Mum and Dad might still be together". Or they may even believe that if their parents somehow had a different or better child, the marriage could have been saved. Such an attitude, however unreasonable to an objective adult mind, is intensely real and reasonable to many children of divorce, causing a deleterious effect on a young person's self-esteem.

Even if they do not blame themselves for their parents' divorce, children may feel different from and less worthy than friends whose families are intact. Because in a divorce, one parent is largely removed from a young person's daily life and the circumstances surrounding the divorce often make it harder for either parent to give enough attention and affection to the children (particularly when they are quite young). Victims of divorce are likely to feel abandoned to some degree. So many even assume that because they have been rejected, they are therefore unlovable.

Parental Resentment

Children may be victims of one parent's resentment towards the other. Such sentiments can be shown at times from that parent's attitude towards a child who either looks like the other parent or even behaves like that person. Statements like "Why do you have to be so much like your mother?" "Why do you behave like your mother?" "I hate you just as I hate your mum", and "You remind me of your mum each time I set my eyes on you" can create a cauldron of anger in a young person. Even in the most amicable situations, the turbulence and activities surrounding the divorce may decrease the amount of time and attention parents are able to give to the family (that is, where they stay together in the same house), which may cause a reaction of frustration and anger in the children.

Certainly, a divorce is likely to cause multiple new resentments and frustration between the divorcing parents which, added to the disaffection that may already have existed, make life more stressful on the children.

Anger/Aggressive Behavior

Aggressive behaviour and getting a model outside their home are also effects on children of a divorced family. Some children tend to be very angry with the whole world and feel unloved and vent their anger on members of the society. This behavioural pattern actually varies from person to person. Some may never exhibit such behavioural traits at all.

However, anger is among the most common responses to parental divorce. A young person may be very angry simply because the divorce disrupts his or her family environment, creating disorder where before there was order. Children may feel angry because they resent being separated from one parent. His or her feelings of abandonment may create anger, or the child may resent being different from friends who still live in intact families.

Physical and financial circumstances may cause anger as well. If the divorce prompts a family to move from a familiar neighbourhood (for instance, where the woman moves with the children), school, church, or a change to less-than-ideal living circumstances, children may respond with anger. Where, for instance, the mother was not working before or worked less hours but is now forced to work or work more hours, children become very angry because they feel that both mother and father are taken away from them for longer periods.

Children, like I mentioned earlier, express their anger in various ways. They may repress it and even feel guilty because they feel angry. They may release it by identifying with others around them or characters in violent movies. They may release it symbolically through passive-aggressive behaviour such as "accidentally" hurting themselves or others. They may also project anger towards others, seeing anger in others' words and behaviour.

Children of a divorce who suppress their anger may suffer heightened stress. They may experience anxiety attacks, which may include sweating, shortness in breath, body tremors, skin irritations, and even a state of severe irrational panic. They may also experience nightmares at night or severe depressions and moodiness during the day.

According to Dr. Richard A. Gardner, the primary purpose of anger is to remove a source of irritation and frustration. When anger is directed at a physical threat, it serves a useful protective purpose, but anger that is directed at divorcing parents (or something more nebulous like the divorce itself, or circumstances) creates far more problems than it solves. Anger that is unresolved may lead to rage and eventually to fury.

Fear

Fear, like anger, is also a common and elemental response to parental divorce. Bowlby in 1969 claimed that the loss of anyone to whom an infant is attached produces an instinctive fear response. Such a loss in older children, such as a loss through divorce, will also frequently produce fear.

Children (both adolescents and preadolescents), in addition to experiencing the same instinctive response, could also, because of their age and relative mental maturity, face fears that are more tangible. They may entertain fears about where they will live, where they will go to school, where they will spend their vacations, etc. They may even fear the reaction of their friends, extended family members, and the church. They may fear total abandonment by one or both parents. They may at times fear losing their grandparents.

Sense of Relief

Those who respond to parental divorce in this way may react by withdrawing and becoming less communicative with their parents or peers. They may suppress or deny their fears. They may become so frustrated by their fears that they respond angrily and begin to lash out emotionally at parents and others. They may experience nightmares or may be more prone to daydream. Some may even be subject to anxiety attacks or panics as with anger.

There are yet other children who actually experience relief not due to selfish and economic gains as earlier stated but actually experience relief when their parents announce plans to divorce or are divorced. Their relief may be occasioned by a variety of factors, but it is most often related to conditions that existed prior to the divorce which may have contributed to the divorce.

Such children say things like "Anything is better than their constant fighting", "I could not wait for him to leave", and "They just never got along". These expressions of relief may be a form of denial intended to mask a young person's pain. Others may use such statements as a means of getting back at their parents for the hurt they have caused their children. For others, however, such statements of relief are a sincere and accurate articulation of their feelings.

Divorce in most cases does not occur out of the blue. It is more often the result of months, perhaps years, of struggles and mistakes. The children in such a family are seldom ignorant of those struggles and mistakes. They may have overheard their parents' arguments. They may have witnessed abuse or suffered abuse themselves. They may have seen their parents fighting themselves. They may even have been aware of one parent's infidelity. As a result, for many children, the threat of a divorce or the divorce itself is welcomed as a promise of relative peace and harmony.

Except the news of a divorce occasionally brings feelings of relief because of prior family conflicts and upheavals, most children usually experience sadness upon learning of their parents' plan to divorce or separate, and they endure occasional moments of sadness as they adjust to the new state of affairs.

Depression

Depression, however, is a prolonged period of sadness, often intense. It is typically characterized by apathy, loss of appetite, loss of interest in and concentration on their studies, loss of ability to enjoy play, loss of ability to enjoy peer relationships, helplessness, hopelessness, irritability, obsessive self-criticism, and withdrawal. Other symptoms may include extreme periods of boredom and low frustration tolerance. Extreme cases may be characterized by self-destructive fantasies and threats of suicide.

Such depression may last for weeks or months in some children. If circumstances other than the divorce itself (like pent-up anger or guilt or the prolonged distress of the custodial parent) contribute to the depression, it may last longer. It should be noted that a certain degree of depression is natural and understandable among the children of divorced parents; long-term depression is not a healthy response.

Substance Abuse

Substance abuse can be defined as an overindulgence in or dependence on an addictive substance, especially alcohol or drugs.

Substance abuse should not be taken lightly by anyone. It occurs when someone uses alcohol, prescription medicine or other illegal substances either too much or in a wrong way. It is not exactly the same as addiction. People with substance abuse issues may be able to quit or make changes of unhealthy behavior.

Addiction on the other hand, is a disease. Those who find themselves in such a situation cannot or find it extremely difficult to stop using the substance even when the condition causes harm to them or their loved ones.

Divorce can cause those involved to resort to substance abuse. Both legal and illegal drugs have chemicals in them that can change how the body and mind of its users work. They can give a pleasurable "high", ease stress or help avoid problems in life. This in my opinion, is an escapist approach which tends to avoid reality and the challenges which can lead to a better life for the spouses; children and everyone affected by a divorce if avoided. It also affects professional growth of the parties of the divorce, the academic performance of their offspring if still in school, and personal relationships due to the problem in communication caused by escapism.

Alcohol, which is one major substance used by most couples having conflicts, affects everyone differently. But if too much is taken and too often, there's a high propensity of injury or accident occurrence. Heavy drinking can result in serious health issues that can affect organs of the body such as the liver, heart or lead to a more serious alcohol disorder.

There's a very high degree of the children from such highly dysfunctional parents due to a divorce becoming victims of what their parents suffer by either becoming substance users themselves, violated or end up in foster homes.

Loneliness

There is also the feeling of loneliness and alienation suffered by adolescent children of divorce. The experience is as a result of the decision taken by the parents. They may feel somewhat estranged from one parent or both. They may feel alienated from their church even when they have experienced no unpleasant or judgemental reaction from church members or leaders. They may feel suddenly distant from their friends. They may feel deserted and rejected by God himself and will frequently wonder how God could allow such a thing to happen to their family.

In the course of such alienation, of course, many children, particularly teenagers, experience bouts of extreme loneliness. They may feel friendless, helpless, and alone. They may think that no one understands what they are going through and what they are feeling. They may withdraw physically to their bedrooms, may withdraw emotionally into fantasy or melancholy, or they may do both.

Sucide

Occasionally, a young person's depression and despair over the broken-up family will become so severe that he or she will threaten or attempt suicide. The victim may view suicide as a way to avoid the pain and grief engendered by the breakup of the family. The person may entertain the hope of "reclaiming" the father's or mother's love and attention by attempting suicide. Suicide may also be (to the child's imagination) a means of communicating how much his or her parents have hurt him or her or a way of making them sorry for their decision. Regardless of the thoughts and emotions behind the threat or attempt, such statements and actions should always be taken seriously and responded to immediately.

There are also academic problems, which are very crucial. Thomas Ewin Smith in 1990 found that adolescent children of single mothers exhibit a lower "academic self-concept" than children living with both biological parents. Furthermore, Shin in 1978 and Hetherington, Camara, and Featherman in 1981 documented that children from two parent families have better grades and higher academic achievement than children in one-parent families. (This may not be true for some children from one-parent families, but it is for most of them.) Such disparity may be the result of many factors. It is more difficult for children to concentrate on schoolwork in times of family turmoil. Slipping grades may be a means of gaining attention or expressing rebellion. Yet some single parents will often find it more difficult to monitor homework. Academic problems may also be an outgrowth of one or more of the problems and emotions mentioned above. School dropout is another aspect of it.

Anti-Social Behavior

Others are the development of antisocial behaviours such as bad manners, poor dressing, teenage pregnancy, sleeping outside the home, smoking, drinking, drug addiction, and prostitution among others.

There is the commonly observed withdrawal syndrome, where children prefer being isolated rather than speaking to other people around them. This could also be traced to the fact that they do not want to be insulted or told things that could remind them of their state as they suffer shame and embarrassment.

In a country like Nigeria, some children from divorced parents could be vulnerable to joining sects like Boko Haram, Daughters of Jezebel, Egbesu Boys (a cult in the Niger Delta Region of Nigeria), etc., and be involved in youths' restiveness and militancy, which are all threats to the nation's security. There have also been found armed robbers whose parents are divorced. I should not be misunderstood as saying that the social vices enumerated apply to only children of divorced parents. It is only a fact that such children are more vulnerable than children of intact marriages where both parents are more likely to watch over the activities of their children.

Some children have misused the separation of parents to deceive them by lying to parents that they are visiting one parent or the other, while they are in reality in other places which they know would not be approved by either parent should they know the truth.

The absence of a father in the home is also a very traumatic aspect that causes negative effects on the children. This is more so when the children attain the age of adolescence. They are more difficult at times to control by a lone resident female parent. Children have been observed to fear their fathers more than their mothers. This may be due to the fact that mothers are more tender and sympathetic towards their children, so they take the tenderness and sympathy for granted and even view this as weakness. This negative behaviour, in some instances, poses a threat to the society.

Stigmatization

There is also the issue of stigmatization when children are referred to as children of a divorce. It is worse when such children attain the age of marriage and want to be married. There have been several instances where parents or family members of the intended spouse whose parents are not divorced oppose marriage to one from a divorced or broken family. This is a common practice in Nigeria. In such situations, the people do not look at the qualities of the young man or woman involved but by judging the person based on his or her family history. They often forget that what happened to the parents' marriage may never happen to the marriage of the person in question. They seldom remember that the party whose parents had a divorce may have learnt through the pains and trauma he or she had passed through and would not want the same to happen to his or her own offspring.

Many also feel stigmatized by their church or neighbourhood because of the family split, and they accept that stigmatization as a reflection of their low worth. Stigmatization may also occur (or be inferred by children or young adults) because of parents' behaviour as a result of the divorce or before the divorce (alcoholism, promiscuity, abusiveness), which can strike a crippling blow to a young person's self-esteem. Economic changes or hardships can also constitute in a young mind evidence of low worth.

Unfortunately, there is another category of victims who may become very sceptical about marriage and will not want to commit their heart to someone whom they presume will eventually treat them the same way their parents' marriage ended; and for this reason, they will rather remain unmarried and without children because they either do not want to have children who could suffer the same fate as they did or because of their religious beliefs of not having children outside the marriage institution. They would rather remain single for life and childless.

Single Parenthood

Some adult children of divorced parents will prefer to remain single and be a lone-parent that has never been married than be married to face a subsequent divorce. It is rather painful to state that having this mindset is not a better approach since the offspring will surely face a more traumatic situation. This situation is more prevalent among female children of divorced parents than among males. It is so with the female adult children who, from observations in their homes, noticed that their mother was seriously violated during the marriage and thrown out of the home—divorced. The children born by the adult child of divorced parents, who refused to marry, may face the challenges of step siblings and may never be accepted as part of that family. This child may end up suffering either the same plight or even worse than what the parent suffered. It is indeed a cycle of ill-fate, and this should be averted.

Nasty Web

Researchers have discovered that some parents a lot of the time end up being worse than what there were prior to the divorce. It is more so when either parent gets himself or herself into another relationship with someone who already had children from either another marriage or relationship. Becoming a stepfather or stepmother poses great problems to either the man or the woman. There are usually frictions between the children and the stepfather or stepmother.

There is also the issue of distrust between members of the new family since the husband or wife may not have implicit trust in the other partner. Worse still is the point where it becomes so nasty when stepfathers sleep with their stepdaughters or stepsons have amorous affairs with step sisters or stepmothers go to bed with their stepsons, stepdaughters with stepsons, etc. Indeed, it is a nasty web.

The solution to this kind of complex situation can only be imagined by you, I guess. Divorce is truly complex and better imagined than experienced. It should, therefore, never be trifled with.

For some divorced persons who may decide to remain unmarried, there is a high degree of moral decadence. In an attempt to spite the other party, he or she may become very promiscuous and flirt around due to lack of self-control. This person cannot in any way be a role model to the children. Some of the children will, if not properly guided by the other parent or a mentor from outside, become victims and follow the poor example of the morally decadent parent.

The effect of divorce on the larger society is obviously terrible. A healthy family, it is said, produces a healthy individual, community, state, nation or society, and world at large. This, simply put, is when the family is in harmony, it naturally flows into the larger society. On the contrary, a family in conflict produces a society full of conflicts and insecurity.

For instance, where most of the families in a particular locality experience lots of problems that either result in divorce or a lone parent society, there is the tendency that such a society will be a reflection of the various families where there is acrimony and frustration all over. This is what is referred to as transferred aggression.

In an unhealthy family in which the children see either of the parents being violated by the other party, they most of the time turn out to be violent because that is the only way of life they see around them. Parents who display irresponsible behaviours before their children have a likelihood of some of their children behaving the same way.

This web which arises from the consequences of divorce can best be described as a *vicious cycle of conflicts*.

The long-term effects of parental divorce may also include fear of betrayal, a fear of commitment, an inability to form close and lasting relationships, and lingering bitterness towards one parent or both or the society.

> 13 Another thing you do: You flood the Lord's
> altar with tears. You weep and wail because he
> no longer looks with favor on your offerings or
> accepts them with pleasure from your hands.

14 You ask, "Why?" It is because the Lord is the witness between you and the wife of your youth. You have been unfaithful to her, though she is your partner, the wife of your marriage covenant.

15 Has not the one God made you? You belong to him in body and spirit. And what does the one God seek? Godly offspring.[a] So be on your guard, and do not be unfaithful to the wife of your youth.

16 "The man who hates and divorces his wife," says the Lord, the God of Israel, "does violence to the one he should protect,"[b] says the Lord Almighty.

So be on your guard, and do not be unfaithful.

Malachi 2:13–16

God hates divorce. Every parent should as much as it is within your power hate divorce to save our children, family and society at large.

CHAPTER SIX

FIX IT

Change is the only constant thing in the world. Man decided in his wisdom to make laws or live a lifestyle that suits him rather than abide by what God meant for him from creation. The disobedience of man is the consequence of man's misfortunes, instabilities, and pains that he experiences in life. The only way out of all his calamities is to go back to his Maker who knows what is best for him. Change. Yes, change is the only answer to man's struggles. Let us return to what marriage should be for a better future for our children and those unborn; let us return, pick the pieces where he fell, and like the prodigal son declare, "I will arise and go to my father". The antidote to divorce is in the Word of God. The solution for a successful marriage cannot be found elsewhere, not even from the parties to any marriage, if they do not depend on the Initiator of marriage. The realization of this fact is the first step to making our marriages work. A man needs a wife to accomplish the purpose for which he was created. Likewise, the wife needs her husband to give her stability and direction as the head to become what God intends her to be. The man and his wife, therefore, need one another to accomplish their purposes here on earth.

God gave man the will to choose right from wrong. If every man, therefore, chooses what is right and the wife in accordance with the Word of God, in submission to her husband, follows what is right, they will then bring up the children with the same fear and reverence for God. This will in turn produce holy and righteous seeds to produce a better and conducive society for all to live in and be happy. What a great society that will be!

Individuals in every family, community, state, or nation of the world should deliberately choose to live right and be nice to one another. The love, joy, and peace that radiate from one family to another will automatically affect his neighbour or vice versa.

Positive change for a positive environment is what the world needs for positive health. Stress is one major killer, say medical researchers. Stress causes lots of illnesses in our society. Most stressors are from within the home rather than from without. Every drunk driver that causes accidents on the road, every man or woman who violates his wife or her husband, every armed robber, every school dropout who later becomes a menace to his society, every young lady or man who parades himself or herself on the streets or hotels as a prostitute, every terrorist killing or causing a threat to society was born and grew in a home at one time or the other, no matter how short-lived this was. If good morals are inculcated into people shortly after they were born, most of the vices we experience today in our various communities and nations might never have been mentioned or reduced.

Effective communication should be practised in our homes. It is not enough just to talk to one's spouse, but one should make sure that the other person understands what you have said, and act upon it, if necessary.

People should get married for the right reasons and not be carried away by infatuations, traditions of men, cultural beliefs, money, age, etc. External family members and friends or third party interference should be minimized or not come into play at all when taking serious family decisions in the home. Spouses should be faithful to one another as well as show mutual respect and understanding towards themselves. When couples are angry over any issue, they should learn to settle their differences without letting their children, domestic staff, relations, and friends know about them. Anger should be short lived and making up very fast should be the utmost thing on their minds. Once anger is built up, communication invariably becomes reduced, distrust sets in, and the soil gradually starts germinating the seed of separation that leads to divorce. The Bible says,

> Be ye angry and sin not: let not the sun go
> down upon your wrath: neither give place to
> the devil. (Ephesians 4:26)

Couples should, before getting married, seek good counsel based on the true teachings of our Lord Jesus Christ as it regards marriage. They should also read good books before and after marriage on how to make their marriages work. Listen to good teachings on radio, televisions, CDs, etc. For nobody can proudly say that he or she knows everything about marriage. It is a school that everyone goes through learning and improving through the help of the Holy Spirit while in it. Nobody graduates from the marriage institution because everyone is a student. It is only those who accept their errors and are willing to make amends on both sides that succeed in this institution. No two marriages are the same, so comparisons should in as much as possible be avoided. However, when couples observe certain good qualities from other marriages, do not be shy to emulate such. There is absolutely nothing wrong in learning what is good from others with a positive attitude rather than a reason for conflicts in families.

Keep unfriendly friends out of your relationship as much as possible. They may be useful to you, if you so believe, in other areas of your life, but definitely not in your marriage. They are full of envy and jealousy. Do not hate them; show them love, but let them know without any apologies that they are not welcome when it concerns your marriage. A broken-down marriage is equal to a broken-down man, a broken-down woman, a broken-down child or children, and a broken-down society. This should be prevented.

Infertility or childlessness could be better handled to prevent divorce. As people whose faith is built upon the Lord Jesus Christ or God, challenges should be handled by couples, amongst other things, through prayers. Prayer must be one basic factor in finding solutions to our problems. Faith-based prayer cannot be said without sufficient knowledge of the Word of God. Couples should, therefore, study the Word of God together to help them in times of crisis. Look at this: "There shall nothing cast their young, nor be barren" (Exodus 23:26).

God honours his Word, and he cannot lie. When Hannah, the mother of Samuel, was barren and mocked by her husband's other wife, Peninnah, she cried to the Lord and he made her fruitful, and she became the mother of not just a son but a prophet of God that feared the Lord. Elizabeth, the mother of John the Baptist, had a similar experience before giving birth to her son John, when man or medical science thought it was over. Not to mention the mother of all nations, Sarah, who was ninety years old when she gave birth to Isaac.

You may be saying those were the Bible days. That is why he is "I AM THAT I AM". He is God yesterday, today, and forever. He is always in the present. What he did before, he is still doing. Age and time is not a barrier with God. Is there anything impossible for him? Certainly nothing. He is a god that makes a way where there is no way. God has made it possible for every couple to have their own children. He is the giver of knowledge.

Marriage, first and foremost, is for companionship and for meeting the needs of one another. God went further to bless man by saying, "Be fruitful, and multiply, and replenish the earth, and subdue it" (Genesis 1:28). "Let the earth bring forth grass, the herb yielding seed and the fruit tree yielding fruits after his kind, whose seed is in itself, upon the earth: and it was so" (Genesis 1:11). Therefore, man brings forth his kind—children. I strongly believe that God in his time blesses his own people even with children to glorify his name. But if for any reason they are unable to have children in the very natural method, God has given knowledge to those in the medical profession to come up with the in vitro fertilization (IVF) process by which babies are born into families. This, I am convinced, is not what any man should boast of to give himself the glory. All glory goes to God. The ovaries and sperm cells used to fertilize the eggs without which there can be no child are created by God. It is also God who has enabled those in the field of medicine to be able to come up with the knowledge that they apply by his wisdom. The Holy Bible says, "If any of you lack wisdom, let him ask of God, that giveth to *all men* liberally, and upbraideth not; and it shall be given him" (James 1:5). Also, in Proverbs 4:7, it is written, "Wisdom is the principal thing; therefore get wisdom: and with all thy getting understanding".

It is quite clear that there is no other source by which any man can acquire or get wisdom except it comes from God who gives to *all men* liberally. (The words "all men" are italicized by me for emphasis.) God gives wisdom to all men to achieve great things in life or do anything for the good of an individual or the larger society. He did not restrict it to those who believe in the faith of our Lord Jesus Christ. No matter the belief or faith of any one or group of persons that came up with the discovery of in vitro fertilization to help couples to be able to multiply and replenish the earth as commanded by God, their wisdom is from God. In the Scriptures, John answered and said, "A man can receive nothing, except it be given from Heaven" (John 3:27). It would be absurd for anyone to solely attribute such discovery and its benefits to anything other than God. There are so-called Christians especially in the developing nations who do not believe that IVF is God's way of blessing couples with children since it is in the strict sense not the natural method of pregnancy for women. This belief is not just faith based but cultural as well. Couples who refuse to benefit from a scientific discovery like the IVF based on their faith, or cultural beliefs when they are desirous of having their own biological children; in my opinion is lacking wisdom. So suffer deprivation, pain, frustration and depression all through their married lives. No wonder the Bible says, "My people are destroyed for lack of knowledge: because thou hast rejected knowledge, I will also reject thee…, seeing thou has forgotten the law of thy God, I will also forget thy children" (Hosea 4:6).

Therefore, couples who are not able to have children can resort to this God-given gift to humanity to be able to have their children rather than going through divorce due to childlessness. Children are an inheritance from God, not science. Science cannot give anyone a child, but God can through science by the wisdom he has imparted to scientists. It is therefore disturbing when Christian marriages break down and end in divorce because they have refused to try the in vitro fertilization method.

Finally, there are those who can become parents by adoption. It does not really matter whether you have biological children of your own or not. Couples can agree to adopt orphaned, abandoned, and poor children into their homes whom they can call their own and raise such less-privileged people in our society who need *parents*. By doing so, you end up becoming parents and making others, who may have ordinarily become problematic to the society because of lack of love and care, become useful and productive people from your very good homes.

Marriage is for mature adults and not for the immature. People should get married only when they are mentally, psychologically, emotionally, and economically developed and balanced and when they are disposed to take responsibilities. Being economically prepared like it happens with most child celebrities in civilized countries such as the USA without any corresponding mental, psychological, and emotional development is one reason for the high level of divorce among celebrities. Money is good, but it is not an answer to mental and emotional stress. Rather, it could be a major stressor if there is lack of maturity in the way it is handled.

In places where young people are forced into early or arranged marriages, either of the spouses in most cases seeks divorce or abandons the other spouse, as the case may be, and remarry because they either did not give their consent at the time of the marriage or did not love the other partner. If children had been born at this point, the effect of such divorce will not only reflect on the parties involved but also on the children and the wider society. Early or immature (untimely marriages) should be discouraged, eliminated, or minimized so that the rate of divorce in our society and some of its inevitable consequences will no longer arise, or at least be reduced.

Couples should seek counsel from leaders in the churches, mosques, other religious leaders where applicable or professional counselling organisations when they strongly sense they need such help. Such steps are positive in avoiding divorce, rather than leaving it till it becomes too late where they see divorce as their only option.

Spouses should take their marriage vows seriously as if the same was made to God. They should realize that it was God who ordained marriage and that he takes the vows made to one another seriously. It is better that vows are not made than breaking them after making them to one another (see Ecclesiastes 5:4). Simply put, it is better that you were never married than to marry and not keep to your marriage vows. See what God says about vows in the book of Ecclesiastes: "When you tell God you'll do something, do it now. God takes no pleasure in *foolish gabble.* Vow it, then do it. Far better not to vow in the first place than to vow and not pay up. Don't let your mouth make a total sinner of you. When called to account, you won't get by with 'sorry, I didn't mean it'. Why risk provoking God to angry retaliation?

But against all illusion and fantasy and empty talk; there is always a rock foundation: Fear God!" (Ecclesiastes 5:5-7).

The words "foolish gabble" means foolish talks. In fact, the King James Version puts it thus: "for he hath no pleasure in *fools:* pay that which thou hast vowed".

In God's eyes, a man or woman who fails to keep the marriage vows is a fool and speaks like one. Couples should not have dreams and fantasies that could result in empty talks, or many words that can result in sin or divorce, but fear God in all their dealings with one another.

I am certain that every religion in one form or the other is hinged on the fear of God. If people truly fear God, then they will treat one another with love and respect and will not want to incur the anger of God by going against his will and having divorces in the society.

Love is a fundamental factor in any marriage. Where there is love, anything is possible to be achieved. Such a key aspect of marriage, therefore, should never be played down. See what the book of 1 Corinthians 13 has to say about love:

> Love never gives up
> Love cares more for others than for self
> Love doesn't want what it doesn't have
> Loves doesn't strut, doesn't have a swelled head,
> Doesn't force itself on others, isn't always "me first"
> Doesn't fly off the handle,
> Doesn't keep score of the sins of others
> Doesn't revel when others grovel, Takes pleasure in the flowering of truth, Puts up with anything.
> Trusts God always
> Always looks for the best,
> Never looks back,
> But keeps going to the end.

This is what love is and does. When people love as husband and wife, you will always look for, or see, the best in your spouse and not always looking out for the things that destroy and pull down. The joy of your spouse should be your joy, and what brings him or her pain should bring you pain. A husband or wife should always think of pleasing or satisfying his or her spouse first before themselves or anyone else.

Be kindhearted, caring, and never give up on your love for him or her. Never look back to the mistakes or faults of your partner; always look for the best. Do not be puffed up or be swollen-headed towards your spouse because of what you may have achieved before or after you got married. Both of you are one flesh, and a head or body cannot be puffed up against herself or himself. It is rather absurd. Keep going and making the best of the relationship, knowing that there is no end to it except through death.

If men love their wives as God has ordained, no woman will be so mad as not to accept such great a depth of love and be submissive to her husband. It is necessary to know at this point that the bible also said that a husband and his wife should submit themselves to one another in the fear of God. No spouse has the right to impose or assert his or her authority over the other no matter the person status in the society. Your spouse is not your maid or staff. He or she became one with you from the moment you said "Yes I Do" to one another. A man who loves his wife or a woman who knows that the husband is her head no matter her standing in the society should never be so heartless to pass their children God has blessed them with through such a trauma as divorce. The love between the parents should naturally flow to the children. How then can one claim to love his or her children when you do not love your spouse?

Are you a person already going through the process of divorce or one whose marriage is already dissolved? Are you already divorced and remarried? Are you a grandparent? It does not matter in whatever category you may find yourself. What has been said so far in this work concerns you too.

Perhaps you are in the process of getting a divorce. You can rethink your decision and ask God to help you be a better wife or husband to your spouse and a great parent to your children. The pain you may be going through, if it is properly handled, will soon become a thing of the past, and you will be happier for it. The pain of today cannot be compared with the stigma, pain, and depression that your children, spouse, and what you will go through in future, once you end the divorce proceedings.

Are you already divorced or even remarried? Then you are the greatest resource person to your children and those you may be connecting with. Be sincere to them. Be open to them. Tell them the truth about how you feel generally about yourself and the environment in which you find yourself. Tell them about some reactions you get from people when they know you are divorced (and maybe remarried, after one or more divorces). If there are resentments of any kind, let them know about such; then advise them based on your experiences.

Will you sincerely want your child, children, or someone you truly love to go through your experiences? Sincerely, I believe that most loving parents, friends, or relatives will not want what has happened to them to occur in the lives of their loved ones.

Are you a grandma or grandpa? You can be a great blessing to your grandchild, who is yet to be married, by counseling him or her on the consequences of divorce so that he or she may not contemplate it either before or after marriage. This will also mean telling him or her how to be a loving and caring husband or a submissive and God-fearing wife who together should become great parents in turn to their children to produce a greater society.

You may say, "I am single and not yet married". In fact, this book is most appropriate for you to guide you early enough against the monster called divorce before you even embark on the journey of marriage.

Finally, are you married and enjoying your marriage? Thank God for you. Do not be too comfortable, for the devil who is the greatest and only enemy to a successful marriage goes about like a roaring lion looking for whom he may devour. Be on the watch. Continue to go by the instructions of the only true manual to a successful marriage—the Holy Bible—and all will be well with you.

Nobody is exempted from reading *The Monster Called Divorce*, for it will open your eyes to what marriage is and the other related issues discussed.

Note that I touched on the aspect of the marriage vows that says "*for better, for worse*" as misinterpreted by some church members. This may be because they lack knowledge and understanding and have misunderstood their pastors. No pastor or any child of God with a good understanding of the scriptures will remain in poverty or sickness. Neither will any pastor wish his members to live in poverty nor sickness. The statement only emphasizes the importance of partners standing by each other in any circumstance. However, I think it should be according to the purpose of God for you.

Religious groups and professional counselling organisations should hold seminars, workshops, advocacy programmes, enlightenment campaigns, radio and television programmes as well as town hall meetings in towns and communities where both married people and single teenagers could be educated on marriage as it ought to be. They should also be taught on the disadvantages of divorce; they should be told that it should not be accepted universally as a way of life. Moral education should be taught in our schools from the primary school level. If possible, counsellors could also be attached to schools to provide proper guidance to students on a variety of issues. Parents, on their part, should live by example for their children to emulate for a better future. If all hands are on deck to sustain the marriage institution and man decides deliberately to go back to the Maker's manual on marriage—the Holy Bible—then the sanity that is so badly needed in our marriages, families, and by extension, the larger society will be achieved.

Finally, brethren, whatsoever things are true, whatsoever things are honest, whatsoever things are just, whatsoever things are pure, whatsoever things are lovely, whatsoever things are of good report, if there be any virtue, and if there be any praise, think on these things. (Philippians 4:8)

REFERENCES

Abekhale, Samson Olorunda Abekhale. "Psychological Effects of Divorce on Family Offsprings in Gboko Local Government Area of Benue State: Counselling Intervention in Strategies." www.transcampus.org/journalsV8No1June 201055.html.

Abrakasa-Ayemieye, Matilda. "Marriage in Nigeria: The Family in Bayelsa State, FIDA Nigeria, Bayelsa State Branch." Proceedings of a workshop held on the 30 and 31 October, 2001, in Yenagoa.

Black's Law Dictionary with Pronunciation. 6th ed. centennial edition (1891-1991).

"Getting Married for the Wrong Reasons." http://www.soenceouragement.org/wrongreasons.htm.

"How to Marry for the Right Reason." http://www.ehow.com/m/ how_2078505_marry-right-reasons.html.

Johnson, Trudy. "Why People Get Married." Posted October 14, 2011. http://www.ehow.com/m/how_2078505_marry-rightreasons.html.

Manser, Martin H, ed. 2004. *The Chambers Thesaurus.* Chambers Harrap Publishers Ltd.

Nwogugu, E. I. 2001. *Family Law in Nigeria.* rev. ed. Nigeria: Heinemann Educational Books Plc.

"Right and Wrong Reasons to Get Married." http://marriage.about.com/cs/engagement/qt/reasons.htm.

- Facts About Robert and Natalie
- Joy Sense and Regis Philbin Marriage Profile.
- Past Issue of Marriage Articles—December, 2011.

The Holy Bible: King James Version, Giant Print Edition. Chattanooga: AMG Publishers.

The New International Webster's Comprehensive Dictionary of the English Language Deluxe Encyclopedic Edition. Typhoon Media Corporation 2010 Edition.

The New International Version/Message Parallel Bible. Michigan, USA: Zondervan.

"Why Do People Get Married?" http://www.lovinghurts. com/2009/05/18/why-do-people-get-married/.

Youngblood, Ronald F., Herbert Lockyer, Sr., F. F. Bruce, and R. K.

Harrison. *Nelson's New Illustrated Bible Dictionary.*

AUTHORS:

Kere Arronse said on May 24, 2009.
Anannyltede said in June 15, 2009.
Brandon Heart said on June 7, 2009.

ABOUT THE AUTHOR

Julie Oguara is a Lawyer and social scientist. A retired Permanent Secretary of the Bayelsa State government of Nigeria. Julie Oguara is the President of The International Centre for Family Care and Rehabilitation. (ICFCR). She is also a motivational speaker.

CPSIA information can be obtained
at www.ICGtesting.com
Printed in the USA
LVHW030435220322
714056LV00009B/433

9 781956 096521